THE GOOD·FOR·YOU
SOUPS
&
STEWS
COOKBOOK

THE GOOD·FOR·YOU
SOUPS
&
STEWS
COOKBOOK

OVER 125 DELICIOUSLY HEALTHFUL RECIPES

Linda Ferrari

PRIMA PUBLISHING
3000 Lava Ridge Court, Roseville, California 95661
(800) 632-8676 • www.primalifestyles.com

PRIMA PUBLISHING and colophon are registered trademarks of Prima Communications, Inc.

Library of Congress Cataloging-in-Publication Data

Ferrari, Linda.
    The good-for-you soups and stews cookbook: over 125 deliciously healthful recipes / Linda Ferrari.
        p.   cm.
    Includes index.
    ISBN 0-7615-2171-2
    1. Soups. 2. Stews. I. Title.
TX757.F47   1994
641.8'13$\frac{1}{M}$ dc20   94-21792
                                                                              CIP

00 01 02 03 HH 10 9 8 7 6 5 4 3 2

Printed in the United States of America

Crock-pot™ is a registered trademark of The Rival Company.

HOW TO ORDER

Single copies may be ordered from Prima Publishing, 3000 Lava Ridge Court, Roseville CA 95661; telephone (800) 632-8676. Quantity discounts are also available. On your letterhead, include information concerning the intended use of the books and the number of books you wish to purchase.

Visit us online at www.primalifestyles.com

*To my longtime friend Jill Presson,
whose helping hands empower me
to explore my culinary fantasies.*

Contents

Acknowledgments

I really appreciate having a place in my book to thank the many people involved in my life who made it possible for me to write this book and others. Taking care of six children, teaching cooking classes, catering, coordinating foreign exchange students, and writing books fills my days and nights. I couldn't do it all without the love and support of my beautiful children, Philip, Cindy, Michelle, Suzy, Carrie, and T.J. My husband, Phil, and my mother, Evelyn Walker, are always stepping in and filling my shoes when needed. My friends Jill Presson, Sherry Davis, Patti Coupe, Sue Perry-Smith, Georgia Bockoven, and Cindy Daniels are there whenever I need them to help me. And, of course, I have to mention my loyal and faithful cooking students who encourage me and give me the confidence I need to continue.

My thanks to Prima's Jennifer Basye Sander for envisioning this journey into the Good-for-You series, and to Karen Blanco and my editor Andi Reese Brady for all the consistent help they gave me. I want to express my appreciation to Lynne Walker at Archetype Book Composition for her enthusiastic response to my problems, and the wonderful job she did on compiling the book; to Linda Dunlavey, Judd Pilossof, and Duane Bibby for the cover design, cover photograph, and illustrations in the book. And last, a very special thanks to my agent, Linda Hayes, for her guidance, understanding, and extreme patience.

Introduction

When I think of my childhood, memories come to mind of summer, when our family headed to local farms to pick fruits and vegetables. Returning home and breathing in the wonderful smells that wafted through the house as big pots of delights bubbled on the stove gave me a sense of comfort and assurance of my mother's caring love. Food has a way of putting its arms around us and making us feel safe and cared for.

What could be a better comfort food than aromatic soups and stews? Soups and stews can be dainty and light or hearty and soul satisfying. No matter what type, soups and stews conjure up a homey, warm feeling in all of us.

Soups and stews are usually easy to prepare, and ingredients can be gathered from whatever you have on hand. With all the fresh vegetables and spices available to us, it is easy to cut the high-fat ingredients out of recipes and still be left with tasty, deliciously flavorful dishes. By adding salad and your favorite bread to a good soup or stew, you have a complete and satisfying meal. Many of these recipes can actually be meals themselves.

The Good-for-You Soups and Stews Cookbook contains many of my family's favorite recipes. Most are new, but some have been passed down from generation to generation. All recipes have been revised to be healthful and low in fat. My hope is that the delicious flavors of these recipes will inspire you to begin your own journey into today's new, healthful approach to cooking.

Crock-pot Adaptations

Because many of us live such fast-paced and busy lives, I have added Crock-pot™ instructions to a few of the recipes. The ingredients are still sautéed before being added to the Crock-pot. If your Crock-pot has a removable stoneware bowl, you may prepare the dish the night before and refrigerate overnight. In the morning, return the stoneware bowl to the base and you are ready to cook.

Liquid is reduced in recipes using the Crock-pot because it does not evaporate in the pot as it does with normal cooking. If you need more liquid toward the end of cooking, just stir in the desired amount. Meat also cooks faster than vegetables with Crock-pot cooking, so you needn't be as concerned about when certain ingredients are to be added. Finally, if you use dried beans, you must soak them overnight and then boil them for ten minutes before you begin. You'll find many more hints by reading the instructions that accompany your Crock-pot.

Freezing Soups and Stews

Most of the soups and stews in this book freeze well. Thus on busy days you can pull out soup or stew in the morning and be able to have a delicious no-fuss dinner.

If you are going to freeze the soup or stew, do not overcook it; remember that warming it up will continue the cooking process. Check the soup or stew for flavor during and after reheating, since some flavoring will be lost in freezing.

Certain ingredients are best added after defrosting, such as cream, sour cream, yogurt, arrowroot or cornstarch, and cottage cheese. These will separate and curdle and become watery during defrosting. Lowfat products do not freeze and reheat well. Other ingredients like broccoli or pasta will be mushy if cooked and then frozen and reheated in the broth; fish will be overdone; and certain potatoes freeze better than others. Plan ahead and remove the portion you want to freeze before adding all the ingredients.

If you cook a large pot of soup and plan to eat it in two or three days, simply refrigerate it. To prevent overcooking, reheat

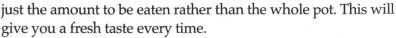

just the amount to be eaten rather than the whole pot. This will give you a fresh taste every time.

Before freezing soups and stews, cool quickly and thoroughly and place in containers, leaving an inch of space to allow for expansion. Most of the recipes in this book can be frozen for up to four months. Stocks can be frozen in all size containers and even in ice cube trays for convenience. They will last up to six months.

A note on nutritional data:
Each recipe includes a per serving nutritional breakdown, including calories, protein, fat, carbohydrate, dietary fiber, sodium, and cholesterol. If a range is given for the number of servings or amount of an ingredient, the breakdown is based on an average of the figures given. Nutritional content may vary depending on the specific brands or types of ingredients used. "Optional" ingredients or those for which no specific amount is stated are not included in the breakdown.

THE GOOD·FOR·YOU
SOUPS
&
STEWS
COOKBOOK

1

Basic Stocks

A good stock is the foundation of all great soups. Stock is easy to make, requires very little attention, and freezes beautifully. On a day when I know I will be home for several hours, I try to make several stocks and freeze them for future use. When freezing stock, use small containers so you can enjoy homemade stock in sauces and other recipes, without having to defrost too much at one time.

I like to bake the solid ingredients that go into some of my stocks first, before I add water and simmer for hours. By doing this the flavors become more intense. Remember, the longer you simmer a stock the more flavor it will have. After removing the solids and straining the liquid, you can reduce the stock until it becomes as concentrated as you like.

Whenever you reduce a stock, it becomes more salty. Because of this it is a good idea not to salt your stock until you have finished devising the recipe in which you are going to be using the stock.

When making homemade stock be sure to cool it in the refrigerator overnight so that you can easily remove the fat that accumulates on the surface. This is called defatting the stock. I

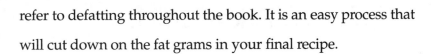

refer to defatting throughout the book. It is an easy process that will cut down on the fat grams in your final recipe.

Chicken Stock

This is a good basic stock to keep on hand.

Makes 3 1/2 quarts

4	to 5-pound chicken
4	chicken wings
3	leeks, white part only, washed and cut in half
2	whole onions, unpeeled and cut in half
2	carrots, washed, unpeeled and cut in half
4	center pieces celery, with leaves attached
4	cloves garlic, peeled
1/4	teaspoon whole peppercorns
4	quarts water
1/3	cup chopped fresh parsley
2	bay leaves
3	sprigs fresh marjoram

Preheat oven to 350°.

Put chicken, wings, leeks, onions, carrots, celery, garlic, and peppercorns into a large roasting pan and cook in oven for 1 1/2 hours. Remove from oven and pour off any fat that has accumulated. Pour 2 quarts of the water into pan and return to oven for 30 minutes. Remove solid ingredients and what liquid is left into a large stock pot. Add parsley, bay leaves, marjoram, and enough water to cover all ingredients, then add the other 2 quarts water. Simmer stock 3 to 4 hours. In the beginning skim off any scum that accumulates on top. Remove solids from

stock and strain the liquid. Cool. Refrigerate overnight and discard any fat that hardens on the surface. Reduce stock to the
concentration you like.

Each serving provides:

12	Calories	1 g	Carbohydrate
1 g	Protein	18 mg	Sodium
0 g	Fat	3 mg	Cholesterol
0 g	Dietary Fiber		

Unbaked Chicken Stock

This stock will not be as dark as chicken stock that is baked first. It will look nicer in clear soups. This is the way my grandmother made clear stock, by using the egg whites and shells.

Makes about 2 1/2 quarts

4	to 5-pound chicken
2	onions, peeled and cut in half
3	leeks, white part only
3	cloves garlic, peeled
4	center pieces celery, with leaves attached
3	carrots, peeled and cut into 2-inch pieces

bouquet garni:
> 1 sprig parsley
> 2 sprigs fresh marjoram
> 2 bay leaves
> 2 teaspoons celery seed
> 4 peppercorns
> 2 sprigs fresh thyme

4	quarts water
2	eggs, whites and shells

Put everything into a large stock pot, except the egg whites and shells, and add water. Cover pot and bring to a boil. Turn to simmer and cook 3 hours.

Strain liquid and return liquid to stock pot. Reduce liquid until desired taste is achieved. Let cool slightly and then whisk the whites and add the shells of two eggs. Bring to a boil and let cook 5 minutes. Let soup cool slightly then strain soup through cheesecloth that has been wet with hot water. If broth is not clear enough, strain again using a new cloth. Season with salt and pepper now or wait until you will be using the stock and then season. Some good seasoning for plain broths are fresh herbs and spices, lemon juice, wine, or brandy.

Each serving provides:

13	Calories	1 g	Carbohydrate
1 g	Protein	20 mg	Sodium
0 g	Fat	3 mg	Cholesterol
0 g	Dietary Fiber		

Beef Stock

When reduced properly this is a rich substantial stock to use in soups, stews, and for all sauces calling for beef.

Makes about 2 1/2 quarts

1	pound brisket
4	beef ribs
1	large veal bone
6	chicken wings
1	large onion, unpeeled and cut in half
2	large carrots, scrubbed not scraped, and cut in half
4	center pieces celery, with leaves attached
1/4	teaspoon peppercorns
6	cloves garlic, peeled
4	quarts water
2	leeks, white part only, washed and cut in half
2	bay leaves
3	sprigs fresh thyme
1/3	cup chopped fresh parsley

Preheat oven to 375°.

Put brisket, ribs, veal bone, wings, onion, carrots, celery, peppercorns, and garlic into a roasting pan and roast 2 hours. Remove from oven and pour off fat that has accumulated in pan. Add 2 quarts of the water to pan and return to oven for 30 minutes. Remove pan again and put all ingredients, including liquid that is left, into a stock pot. Add leeks, bay leaves, thyme, and parsley. Cover contents of pan with water and add 2 quarts water. Simmer stock 3 hours. In the beginning skim off any scum that accumulates on the surface.

Strain and refrigerate overnight. Discard any hardened fat that rises to the surface. You can now reduce stock to the concentration you prefer.

❖

Each serving provides:

17	Calories	1 g	Carbohydrate
2 g	Protein	18 mg	Sodium
1 g	Fat	5 mg	Cholesterol
0 g	Dietary Fiber		

Vegetable Stock

If you do not care if your vegetable stock is clear, potatoes, tomatoes, sweet potatoes, turnips, and squash are just a few of the other vegetables that make a beautiful and rich-tasting stock. When this vegetable stock is reduced, it is a wonderful way to enrich many dishes—with only a trace of fat.

Makes 2 quarts when reduced

2	onions, unpeeled and cut in half
4	carrots, scrubbed and cut in half
2	large tomatoes, cut in half
1	bunch celery, cut in half
2	peppers, seeded and cut in half
3	parsnips, unpeeled and cut in half
6	cloves garlic, peeled
1/4	teaspoon peppercorns
	vegetable spray
4	quarts water
2	leeks, white part only, washed and cut in half
2	bay leaves
1/2	cup chopped fresh parsley
3	fresh sprigs thyme
3	fresh sprigs tarragon
3	large fresh basil leaves
2	sprigs fresh marjoram

Preheat oven to 350°.

Put onions, carrots, tomatoes, celery, peppers, parsnips, garlic, and peppercorns into a roasting pan that has been sprayed with vegetable spray. Bake 40 minutes. Remove from oven, add 2 quarts water, and return to oven for 15 minutes. Put ingredients and liquid from roasting pan into a stock pot. Add leeks, bay leaves, parsley, thyme, tarragon, basil, marjoram, and remaining water to vegetables. Simmer 1 hour. Strain and reduce to concentration you prefer.

Each serving provides:

38	Calories	8 g	Carbohydrate
1 g	Protein	3 mg	Sodium
0 g	Fat	0 mg	Cholesterol
0 g	Dietary Fiber		

Fish Stock

If you are in a hurry for a recipe calling for fish stock, substitute bottled clam juice.

Makes about 7 cups

1	pound fish trimmings (heads, tails, bones)
1	pound good white fish
1	onion, peeled and quartered
2	carrots, unpeeled and cut in half
2	ribs celery, with leaves attached
2	3-inch pieces lemongrass
1/2	cup fresh sorrel
1/4	cup chopped fresh parsley
2	cloves garlic, peeled
1/4	teaspoon white peppercorns
1	cup vermouth
	8-ounce bottle clam juice
6	cups water

Put all ingredients into a stock pot. Add water and cook 30 minutes. Discard solids and strain. Refrigerate or freeze until ready to use.

❖

Each serving provides:

27	Calories	1 g	Carbohydrate
1 g	Protein	1 mg	Sodium
0 g	Fat	0 mg	Cholesterol
0 g	Dietary Fiber		

FRUIT STOCK

This may be the first time you have heard of a fruit stock. Besides using this stock as a base for fruit soups, I will also use this to enhance some of the stews. You can obtain a rich flavor, similar to what butter emits, when you add a small amount of concentrated fruit stock to your stew. Choose just one or a combination of fruits to use.

Makes 2 quarts

2	pounds fruit (prunes, plums, peaches, apricots, cherries, apples, pineapple, pears, or berries)
1/4	cup chopped onion
	juice of 1 lemon
	juice of 1 orange
3	tablespoons sugar
1/4	cup white wine
6	cups water

Peel fruits like peaches. (Do not bother to pit.) Put fruits, onion, lemon juice, orange juice, sugar, wine, and water into a pot. Cover and simmer 30 minutes. Strain stock and reduce to concentrate if desired. Freeze in 1/2-cup containers.

❖

Each serving provides:

59	Calories	14 g	Carbohydrate
0 g	Protein	8 mg	Sodium
0 g	Fat	0 mg	Cholesterol
0 g	Dietary Fiber		

Oriental Noodle Soup 19

Gingery Crab Soup 20

Lemon Soup 22

Light Tomato and Wine Soup
with Basil Dumplings 24

Celeriac and Carrot Soup 26

Spinach and Mushroom Soup 27

Fish Soup with Ginger and Lime 28

Clear Soup with Painted Pasta 30

2

Clear
Soups

When I refer to clear soups, I am speaking of beautiful, clear stocks, in which you can easily see the few solid ingredients that are in the soup. The solid ingredients are more for looks, while the real pleasure of the soup comes from the delightful stock.

A secret in keeping your stock clear and not having it cloud up is to cook solid ingredients in a separate pan. When they are cooked, add them to the clear stock.

These soups make a beautiful and interesting first course. They are light and luscious, and fit nicely into a menu made up of many courses.

Oriental Noodle Soup

I love small serving bowls of this delightful soup before an Oriental meal.

Makes 8 servings

8	cups unbaked chicken stock, defatted (see page 8)
2	tablespoons lite soy sauce
1	tablespoon rice vinegar
1/2	cup dry sherry
1	tablespoon mirin
1/2	teaspoon chili oil
4	cups water
2	green onions, slivered
1/4	cup *each* slivered carrot and snow peas
2	ounces bean thread noodles, soaked in hot water 15 minutes then cut into 2-inch lengths
1/4	teaspoon white pepper
1/2	teaspoon grated ginger root

Put chicken stock, soy sauce, rice vinegar, sherry, mirin, and chili oil into a stock pot. Bring to a simmer and cook 10 minutes.

In a separate pan put 4 cups of water and simmer green onions, carrot, snow peas, and noodles for 5 minutes. Drain and rinse. Add noodle and vegetable mixture, white pepper, and ginger to clear broth and warm for 5 minutes.

❖

Each serving provides:

57	Calories	9 g	Carbohydrate
1 g	Protein	173 mg	Sodium
1 g	Fat	3 mg	Cholesterol
1 g	Dietary Fiber		

Gingery Crab Soup

It is essential to use fresh crab so you can have nice chunks of crab in the soup.

Makes 8 servings

8	cups vegetable stock (see page 12)
1/3	cup fish sauce
	juice of 2 lemons
	a few drops of chili oil

bouquet garni:
      1/2-inch piece fresh ginger
      1/2 small onion, peeled and left in 1 piece
      5 large whole leaves of Chinese basil (if not available, use 3 large basil leaves and 2 1-inch pieces fresh anise)
      shell of 1 egg

2	green onions, thinly sliced
1	clove garlic, minced
1/3	cup minced bok choy
2	tablespoons minced celery
1	teaspoon sesame oil
12	ounces fancy crab meat
1	tablespoon soy sauce
2	teaspoons oyster sauce
1/4	teaspoon grated fresh ginger
1/4	teaspoon minced lemongrass
1	egg
24	wonton wrappers
1	egg white mixed with 3 tablespoons water

Pour vegetable stock, fish sauce, lemon juice, chili oil, and bouquet garni of spices and herbs into a stock pot. Let mixture simmer 30 minutes. Remove bouquet and discard. Strain soup
through 3 layers of cheesecloth.

Sauté green onions, garlic, bok choy, and celery in a small
pan with sesame oil until vegetables just start to turn color. Mix
in crab, soy sauce, oyster sauce, ginger, and lemongrass until
well combined. Mix in egg and set mixture aside.

Put 1 heaping teaspoon crab mixture in the center of each
wonton. Brush edges of wrappers with the egg white mixture.
Fold wrapper over and press edges together. Repeat with all 24
wontons.

Slowly simmer soup then add wontons. Do not let soup boil,
but simmer until wontons are cooked, about 5 to 8 minutes.
Serve soup with 3 wontons in each bowl.

❖

Each serving provides:

198	Calories	29 g	Carbohydrate
15 g	Protein	1034 mg	Sodium
3 g	Fat	70 mg	Cholesterol
1 g	Dietary Fiber		

LEMON SOUP

*If you cannot find lemon pasta in your gourmet food stores or kitchen-
ware shops, it is really easy to make. If you have a food processor it
takes no time at all; if not, it doesn't take much longer with a wooden
spoon and bowl. The results of homemade pasta are well worth the
effort.*

Makes 4 servings

1	tablespoon honey
1	tablespoon water
1	teaspoon butter
1/3	cup minced onion
4	cups water
1/4	cup lemon juice
2	teaspoons soy sauce
1/4	cup white wine
1/3	cup slivered sorrel or spinach
1/3	cup very thinly julienned carrot
1	cup cooked lemon pasta (see below)
	salt and white pepper to taste

Put honey, water, butter, and onion into a nonstick pan and
cook slowly until all liquid evaporates. Put onion mixture, together with water, lemon juice, soy sauce, wine, sorrel, and carrot into a stock pot. Cook 20 minutes. Add pasta and cook 5
minutes more. Season with salt and pepper.

Lemon Pasta

1	cup flour
2	egg whites
1/4	cup lemon juice
	rind of 1 lemon
1	teaspoon salt

To make pasta, put flour, egg whites, lemon juice, lemon rind, and salt into a bowl or food processor. Process or stir until mixture just sticks together. Remove pasta and roll together. Cut off pieces about the size of a golfball and roll thin with a rolling pin or put through a hand-cranked pasta machine. Cut into thin noodles. Let dry at least 15 minutes or overnight and store in airtight containers.

Each serving provides:

123	Calories	22 g	Carbohydrate
6 g	Protein	522 mg	Sodium
2 g	Fat	3 mg	Cholesterol
2 g	Dietary Fiber		

Light Tomato and Wine Soup with Basil Dumplings

This is a lovely soup, and it is best made in summer when tomatoes are at their best. It must be made with juicy ripe tomatoes for a really good flavor. I like to put up 100 quarts of tomatoes each summer so that I can recapture the fresh taste of tomatoes all year long in my soups, stews, and sauces.

Makes 8 servings

1/2	cup minced onion
1/4	cup slivered fresh basil
3	tablespoons plus 3 cups chicken stock, defatted (see page 6)
1/2	cup dry white wine
5	medium whole tomatoes, peeled and puréed
1	teaspoon sugar
1	tablespoon tomato paste
1	tablespoon lemon juice
	salt and pepper to taste

Sauté onion and basil in 3 tablespoons of stock until stock evaporates. Add the broth, wine, tomato purée, sugar, tomato paste, and lemon juice. Cook 10 minutes. Season with salt and pepper to taste.

Dumplings

1	cup flour
1	teaspoon salt
2	tablespoons chopped fresh basil

1	tablespoon chopped fresh parsley
1	teaspoon baking powder
2	tablespoons fat free cream cheese
3	cloves garlic, minced
1/4	cup egg substitute
3/4	cup nonfat milk
2	tablespoons Parmesan cheese

Mix flour, salt, basil, parsley, and baking powder. Using a pastry blender, cut the cream cheese into the flour mixture. Add garlic, egg substitute, milk, and Parmesan cheese. Blend until ingredients are just wet. Reduce soup to a slow simmer. Drop tablespoons of dumplings on the top of the soup. Cover and simmer 20 minutes, without removing lid.

Each serving provides:

116	Calories	21 g	Carbohydrate
6 g	Protein	535 mg	Sodium
1 g	Fat	3 mg	Cholesterol
2 g	Dietary Fiber		

Celeriac and Carrot Soup

Celeriac is a delicious and versatile vegetable.

Makes 6 servings

4	cups water
1	tablespoon lemon juice
1/2	teaspoon salt
1	teaspoon sugar
1	cup peeled and julienned celeriac
1	cup peeled and julienned carrot
6	cups unbaked chicken stock, defatted (see page 8)
2	green onions, slivered
	salt and fresh ground pepper to taste
1	tablespoon chopped fresh tarragon

Bring water, lemon juice, salt, and sugar to a boil. Add celeriac and carrot and cook 8 minutes. Drain.

Put stock and green onions into a saucepan and heat. Add salt and pepper to taste.

Put vegetables into a soup bowl and add stock. Sprinkle each bowl with a little tarragon.

Each serving provides:

33	Calories		6 g	Carbohydrate
2 g	Protein		365 mg	Sodium
0 g	Fat		3 mg	Cholesterol
1 g	Dietary Fiber			

Spinach and Mushroom Soup

My son T.J. loves spinach, so this is one of his favorite soups.

Makes 6 servings

4 1/2   cups unbaked chicken stock, defatted (see page 8)
2   cups fresh white mushrooms, thinly sliced
2   tablespoons chopped chives
2   tablespoons lemon juice
1/2   cup dry sherry
1   cup fresh spinach leaves, stems removed
        salt and white pepper to taste

Take 1/2 cup of the stock and cook the mushrooms and chives in it until stock evaporates. While the mushrooms are cooking, put the rest of the stock, lemon juice, and sherry into a stock pot and let cook for 10 minutes. When mushrooms are done add to the stock along with the spinach. Cook uncovered until spinach is cooked. Taste and season with salt and pepper.

❖

Each serving provides:

31	Calories	3 g	Carbohydrate
2 g	Protein	160 mg	Sodium
0 g	Fat	2 mg	Cholesterol
1 g	Dietary Fiber		

Fish Soup with Ginger and Lime

This flavorful soup sets well with mild sea bass.

Makes 4 servings

1	cup plus $3/4$ cup fish stock (see page 14)
2	cups chicken stock, defatted (see page 6)
$1/4$	cup white wine
$1/4$	cup slivered fresh sorrel
1	teaspoon fresh dill
2	teaspoons coriander
$1/2$	teaspoon turmeric
2	tablespoons lime juice
1	teaspoon slivered lime rind (reserve a little for garnish)
2	whole cloves garlic, peeled
1	inch fresh ginger, thinly sliced
2	teaspoons lite soy sauce
1	tablespoon Worcestershire sauce
2	slices of lime
$1/2$	teaspoon *each* salt and pepper
1	pound sea bass

Combine 1 cup of fish stock with chicken stock, wine, sorrel, dill, coriander, turmeric, and lime juice in a pan and heat. Put lime rind in a pan with a little water and boil 2 minutes. Drain and reserve.

In a separate pan, put rest of fish stock, garlic, ginger, soy sauce, Worcestershire sauce, sliced lime, salt, pepper, and fish.

Steam, covered, 5 to 8 minutes depending on the thickness of the bass. Remove the fish and put into soup bowls. Ladle stock over fish and sprinkle each dish with a little slivered lime rind.

❖

Each serving provides:

146	Calories	3 g	Carbohydrate
23 g	Protein	92 mg	Sodium
3 g	Fat	51 mg	Cholesterol
1 g	Dietary Fiber		

Clear Soup with Painted Pasta

If you don't want to make your own pasta, you can use wontons.
Brush one side of a wonton wrapper with water and lay some flat herb
leaves on it. Cover with another wonton. Then roll over the wontons
with a rolling pin a couple of times. (Be sure you have moistened the
wontons enough or they will separate during cooking.) The recipe I
am giving for homemade pasta makes quite a bit. It has so many uses
and looks so beautiful that you will want to freeze the extra between
wax paper for another time.

Makes 6 servings of soup and extra pasta

Clear Soup

8	cups unbaked chicken stock, defatted (see page 8)
1/2	cup Gewurztraminer wine
	salt and white pepper to taste
1	carrot, thinly julienned, cooked in 2 cups water with 1 teaspoon sugar for garnish
1/2	recipe painted pasta

Painted Pasta

1	cup flour
3	large egg whites
1/2	teaspoon salt
2	teaspoons virgin olive oil
1/2	egg shell of water
1/8	cup flat-leafed herbs (sorrel, Italian parsley, basil, etc.)

Cook stock down to 6 cups. Add wine and cook 10 minutes.
Cook noodles in separate boiling water until done. Add to

stock and season with salt and pepper. Ladle into bowls and sprinkle with a few julienned carrots.

You can make noodles in a processor or by hand in a bowl. Add all ingredients, except herbs, and mix well. Knead well, cover with an inverted bowl, and let sit 10 minutes. Roll out dough on a counter or in a pasta machine until very thin. Lay out 2 strips of pasta. Brush with water and lay some flat-leafed herbs on 1 of the pieces of pasta. Cover with the other piece of pasta and roll together until well sealed, either with a rolling pin or through a hand-cranked pasta machine.

Each serving provides:

108	Calories	11 g	Carbohydrate
4 g	Protein	373 mg	Sodium
4 g	Fat	4 mg	Cholesterol
1 g	Dietary Fiber		

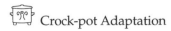

 Crock-pot Adaptation

3

Bisques, Chowders, and Gumbos

❖

The anticipation of waiting to dive into a bowl of thick, luscious soup is sometimes unbearable. Bisques, chowders,
and gumbos are so filling and nourishing, they are definitely a
satisfying meal in themselves. I love to cook these kinds of soups
because you can experiment with the ingredients and change
them a little each time you make them.

Distinguishing these soups can be confusing, so I will try to
define them for you. Through the years, creative cooking always
alters the fundamentals of past definitions, but that is what
makes cooking so fascinating.

A *bisque* is a rich, creamy soup that usually starts off with a
roux for its base. It contains a mirepoix (a combination of diced
onion, carrots, and celery used to flavor stocks, stews, and
sauces) of sautéed vegetables or shellfish that are sautéed in their
shells. Then shellfish, fish, meat, or vegetables are added. It is
often flavored with wine or brandy, is light on spices, and is
made with lots of butter and cream. We are going to cut the fat in
this soup by thickening it with grated or mashed potatoes or
puréed rice or vegetables. We will add nonfat milk or evaporated lite milk in place of the cream. Your bisque will have a very
rich taste and texture without the high fat.

A *chowder* is another thick soup that contains potatoes, lots of onions, vegetables, salt pork, fish, and shellfish or chicken. Potato is used to thicken this soup instead of roux, as with a bisque. It contains milk or cream and is also light on seasonings. Chowders are great fun to make and can be individualized easily. To lessen the fat with chowders we will omit the salt pork, replacing it with liquid smoke flavoring, and replace the cream with nonfat milk or evaporated lite milk.

A *gumbo* is a thick soup that is sometimes referred to as a stew. It is very spicy, dark in color, and extremely aromatic. It has a base of thick, browned roux, includes a thick vegetable sauté, tomatoes, and greens, and is additionally thickened with filé powder (ground sassafras leaves) or okra. It contains vegetables, meat, or seafood and is usually served on rice. An important part of gumbo is the browned roux, which gives gumbo its rich brown color. We will lessen the fat content of the roux and still enjoy this soul-satisfying dish.

Since the fat is reduced in these soups, I have found it helpful to cook them in nonstick stock pans. It eliminates the worry of scorching the soup.

Garlicky Potato Bisque

The aroma of this delightful soup makes it hard to resist.

Makes 8 servings

2	heads garlic, roasted
	olive oil spray
3	tablespoons plus 4 cups chicken stock, defatted (see page 6)
3	leeks, white part only, sliced
2	teaspoons butter
2	tablespoons flour
2	cups nonfat milk
1	cup mashed potatoes
3	cups diced and peeled russet potatoes
1/3	cup chopped cilantro
1	12-ounce can lite evaporated milk
	salt and pepper to taste

To roast the garlic, cut tops off the garlic heads. Put garlic into a small ovenproof dish, sprinkle with a little salt and pepper, and spray the top of the garlic with olive oil spray. Pour 3 tablespoons of chicken stock over the garlic and cover dish tightly with foil. Put into a 300° oven for 1 1/2 hours. When garlic is done, remove, let cool slightly, squeeze garlic out, and mash. Reserve.

Sauté leeks in butter for 2 minutes. Add 2 tablespoons flour that has been mixed with 1/4 cup hot water and blend. Whisk in 4 cups of chicken stock and milk. Add mashed potatoes, diced potatoes, roasted garlic purée, and cilantro. Cook 40 minutes. Reduce heat to simmer and blend in evaporated milk. Season with salt and pepper to taste.

Each serving provides:

177	Calories	33 g	Carbohydrate
9 g	Protein	330 mg	Sodium
2 g	Fat	8 mg	Cholesterol
2 g	Dietary Fiber		

Crock-pot Adaptation

Roast garlic the night before or before starting the recipe. Follow the recipe above until time to cook for 40 minutes. Instead, put mixture into Crock-pot and cook on low 7 to 8 hours or on high 3 to 4 hours. Turn temperature down to low (if not already using low temperature) and add evaporated milk, salt, and pepper. Blend well and let cook 15 minutes more.

Corn and Tomato Bisque with Pepper Purée

When the farmers' markets are full of corn and fresh peppers I am always looking for new ways to use them. It is very easy to char peppers; the resulting flavor is wonderful.

Makes 12 servings

1	onion, minced
2	leeks, white part only, sliced
3	cloves garlic, minced
2	teaspoons butter
1/3	cup flour
1	cup boiling water
6	cups chicken broth, defatted (see page 6)
2	cups nonfat milk
1	to 2 teaspoons liquid smoke flavoring
6	fresh cobs of corn, broken in half
5	fresh tomatoes, peeled, seeded, and diced
4	potatoes, peeled, cut into 1/2 -inch dice
2	carrots, peeled and diced
2	teaspoons dried basil
1	teaspoon dried thyme
2	tablespoons chopped fresh parsley
1/2	teaspoon hot sauce (or to taste)
2	bay leaves
1	cup slivered fresh spinach
1/2	cup small diced celeriac
3	tablespoons sherry
	salt and pepper to taste
1	heaping teaspoon pepper purée (see below)

Pepper Purée

1   large green or red pepper, charred
1   tablespoon nonfat sour cream
1   teaspoon reduced-calorie mayonnaise
1   tablespoon fresh chopped basil
       salt and pepper to taste

Sauté onion, leeks, and garlic in butter until soft. Whisk flour and water together and add to onions. Add broth, milk, and smoke flavoring and stir to totally blend in flour mixture. Cook 10 minutes. Add corn cobs, tomatoes, potatoes, carrots, basil, thyme, parsley, hot sauce, and bay leaves. Cook 40 minutes. Discard bay leaves and remove cobs of corn. Cut corn from cobs and return corn kernels to soup. Using a spoon, scrape the cobs and add milky substance to soup. Discard cobs. Cook soup 15 minutes more. Add spinach, celeriac, and sherry and cook 8 minutes more. Season with salt and pepper and serve each bowl with pepper purée.

Char pepper by putting pepper under the broiler until charred on all sides, or char on open flame of stove. When pepper is blackened put into a plastic bag and zip closed. Let sit 10 minutes. Remove and peel.

To make pepper purée: Put the rest of the ingredients into a blender and purée. Heat up mixture to serve on soup.

Each serving provides:

150	Calories	30 g	Carbohydrate
5 g	Protein	336 mg	Sodium
2 g	Fat	4 mg	Cholesterol
4 g	Dietary Fiber		

SWEET POTATO CURRY BISQUE

This is a scrumptious soup to serve for Thanksgiving, but it is so good you should make it all year round.

Makes 10 servings

1	cup diced onion
1/2	cup shredded carrot
1	celery stalk, minced
	butter-flavored vegetable spray
3	tablespoons flour mixed with 3/4 cup hot water
2	pounds sweet potato, peeled and cut into 1/2-inch dice
1	pound parsnips, peeled and diced
1	to 1 1/2 tablespoons curry powder
2	teaspoons dried thyme
2	tablespoons fresh parsley
5	cups chicken broth
1	cup nonfat milk
1/2	teaspoon white pepper
1/4	cup good brandy
3/4	cup lite evaporated milk
	salt to taste

Sauté the onion, carrot, and celery in a nonstick pan sprayed with butter-flavored vegetable spray until onion is soft.

Put flour and hot water in a bowl and whisk until flour is completely mixed in, with no lumps of flour left. Add flour mixture, 1 pound of the sweet potatoes (save the other pound to add later), parsnips, curry powder, thyme, parsley, broth, milk, and pepper to vegetables. Stir well to incorporate flour mixture. Cook for about 30 minutes, until potatoes are done. Purée mixture. Return to pan and add the other pound of sweet potatoes. Cook another 30 minutes or until these potatoes are soft. Stir in brandy and evaporated milk and season with salt if necessary. Turn to a low simmer and warm for 5 minutes.

Each serving provides:

164	Calories	33 g	Carbohydrate
5 g	Protein	198 mg	Sodium
1 g	Fat	3 mg	Cholesterol
4 g	Dietary Fiber		

Lemony Seafood Bisque

This bisque is a seafood lover's delight!

Makes 12 servings

1	pound shrimp, peeled (reserve peelings)
1	crab leg, cut into 3 pieces
3	teaspoons olive oil
3	cloves garlic, minced
2	shallots, minced
3	tablespoons flour
4	cups fish stock (see page 14)
1	carrot, shredded
1	stalk celery, minced
1	yellow pepper, minced
1/4	cup chicken broth, defatted (see page 6)
1 1/2	cups grated cooked potato
1/2	cup sorrel
1	tablespoon fresh parsley
1/2	teaspoon dried dill
1	tablespoon lemon rind
1/4	cup lemon juice
2	cups white wine
1	pound lobster meat
12	ounces crab meat
1	cup lite evaporated milk
1	teaspoon white pepper (or to taste)
	salt to taste

Sauté shrimp peelings and crab leg in olive oil, slowly, for 10 minutes in a nonstick stock pan. Remove peelings and crab leg pieces, put into a piece of cheesecloth, and tie with kitchen string. Reserve.

Sauté garlic and shallots in same pan for 1 minute. Sprinkle flour over shallots and garlic and stir until white from flour does not show. Whisk in fish stock until smooth. Set aside. Add carrot, celery, and pepper and cook on low heat in chicken broth until vegetables are soft and broth has evaporated. Add tied-up peels and crab pieces, potatoes, sorrel, parsley, dill, lemon rind, lemon juice, fish stock mixture, and wine to pot. Cook slowly for 30 minutes. Remove cheesecloth and discard. Cut shrimp and lobster into small dice. Add shrimp, lobster, and crab meat and cook slowly until shrimp and lobster are done. Turn heat to low, stir in evaporated milk, and cook slowly for 3 more minutes. Add pepper and salt to taste.

❖

Each serving provides:

173	Calories	13 g	Carbohydrate
21 g	Protein	416 mg	Sodium
2 g	Fat	86 mg	Cholesterol
1 g	Dietary Fiber		

Vegetarian Chowder

I have always bought cranberry beans from farmers' markets, but many grocery stores also carry them. If you cannot find them, substitute pink beans.

Makes 12 servings

1/2	cup minced onion
2	cloves garlic, minced
1	tomato, peeled, seeded, and chopped
5	cups vegetable stock (see page 12)
3	cups nonfat milk
4	medium potatoes, peeled and diced small
1/2	pound green beans, cut into 1-inch pieces
2	carrots, peeled and diced
3	stalks celery, sliced
2	cups cooked cranberry beans
1	cup corn kernels
2	fennel bulbs, diced
1	cup diced zucchini
1	tablespoon minced fresh sage
1	tablespoon minced fresh marjoram
1	tablespoon fresh rosemary
1	tablespoon minced fresh parsley
1	teaspoon fresh ground pepper
	salt to taste
2	tablespoons arrowroot mixed with 3 tablespoons water (optional)

Put onion, garlic, and tomato into a nonstick stock pan and cook slowly until liquid from tomato is almost evaporated. Add stock, milk, potatoes, green beans, carrots, celery, cranberry beans, and corn. Cook 40 minutes. Add fennel, zucchini, sage, marjoram, rosemary, parsley, pepper, and salt. Cook 12 minutes more. Thicken with arrowroot mixture if you prefer a thicker chowder.

Each serving provides:

164	Calories	34 g	Carbohydrate
7 g	Protein	198 mg	Sodium
1 g	Fat	1 mg	Cholesterol
4 g	Dietary Fiber		

Turkey Chowder

This is the soup we anxiously wait for the day after Thanksgiving.

Makes 12 servings

1	turkey carcass
	water to cover
1	whole onion, peeled and cut in half
4	whole celery stalks, with leaves attached
1	carrot, scrubbed and cut in fourths
4	whole cloves garlic
1	bay leaf
8	cups turkey stock
2	cups nonfat milk
5	medium potatoes, peeled and diced (or leftover mashed potatoes)
3	carrots, peeled and diced
3	celery stalks, diced
1	cup frozen lima beans
2	ounces small shell noodles
2	cups slivered fresh chard
1	cup fresh or frozen peas
	turkey meat off carcass
1/4	cup fresh parsley
1	teaspoon dried marjoram
1	teaspoon fresh pepper
	salt to taste
1	cup lite evaporated milk
2	tablespoons arrowroot mixed with 4 tablespoons water (optional)

Totally remove any skin from the turkey carcass. Put turkey into a stock pot and cover with water. Add onion, celery, carrot, garlic, and bay leaf and cook 2 hours, covered.

Remove carcass and strain liquid. Remove as much turkey meat as you can from the carcass and save for chowder. Refrigerate turkey stock overnight and in the morning remove fat that accumulates on top.

Put turkey stock, milk, potatoes, carrots, and celery into a soup pot. Cook 30 minutes. Add lima beans, noodles, chard, peas, turkey meat, parsley, marjoram, and pepper to the soup and cook 20 minutes. Remove from heat, season with salt if necessary, and stir in evaporated milk. Return to heat, stir well, and put on low heat for 3 minutes. Do not let soup boil. Thicken with arrowroot mixture if you want a thicker chowder.

❖

Each serving provides:

183	Calories	28 g	Carbohydrate
14 g	Protein	264 mg	Sodium
2 g	Fat	21 mg	Cholesterol
2 g	Dietary Fiber		

Green Bean and Zucchini Chowder

Once I plant beans and zucchini I have to invent lots of ways to use up my ample supply. This is a great way.

Makes 10 servings

2	leeks, white part only, sliced
1	medium onion, chopped
2	cloves garlic, chopped
1/2	inch ginger, minced
1/4	teaspoon red pepper flakes
2	teaspoons butter
1/2	cup sherry
3	large potatoes, peeled and diced large
2	carrots, peeled and diced
1	stalk celery, sliced
2	large tomatoes, peeled and diced
1 1/2	cups green beans, cut in 1/2-inch lengths
1/4	cup chopped fresh celery leaves
1/2	teaspoon liquid smoke flavoring
6	cups chicken stock, defatted, or vegetable stock (see pages 6, 12)
2	cups nonfat milk
1	teaspoon white pepper
1 1/2	cups diced zucchini, green or yellow
	salt to taste
1/2	cup lite evaporated milk
	chopped, fresh celery leaves for garnish

Put leeks, onion, garlic, ginger, red pepper flakes, butter, and sherry into a pan and cook until liquid evaporates. Add potatoes, carrots, celery, tomatoes, green beans, celery leaves, smoke flavoring, stock, milk, and pepper in pan and cook 40 minutes. Add zucchini and salt to taste and cook for 12 minutes longer. Stir in evaporated milk and cook over very low heat for 1 minute more, just to blend. Sprinkle with fresh celery leaves and serve.

Each serving provides:

106	Calories	19 g	Carbohydrate
5 g	Protein	215 mg	Sodium
1 g	Fat	5 mg	Cholesterol
2 g	Dietary Fiber		

Sprouting Onion Chowder

There are lots of steps in creating this luscious soup, but it is well worth the effort.

Makes 12 servings

1	head garlic, roasted
	vegetable spray
3	tablespoons plus ³/₄ cup beef stock, defatted (see page 10)
1¹/₂	pounds sweet potatoes, peeled and cut into ¹/₂-inch dice
1	pound pearl onions
1	teaspoon sugar
2	tablespoons tomato paste
2	cups diced yellow onions
3	leeks, white part only, sliced
3	shallots, chopped
2	teaspoons unsalted butter
10	cups beef stock, defatted (see page 10)
3	medium white potatoes, diced
2	carrots, diced
2	stalks celery, diced
1	teaspoon *each* dried marjoram, savory, and thyme
	salt and pepper to taste

Roast garlic by cutting top off head garlic. Put garlic into a small ovenproof bowl (custard cups work well). Spray top of garlic with vegetable spray and add 3 tablespoons of the beef stock. Cover tightly with foil and put into a 300° oven for 1¹/₂ hours. Squeeze out garlic and mash. Set aside.

Boil sweet potatoes in salted water until tender. Mash up half the potatoes. Reserve the rest.

Boil some water and throw in pearl onions. Let cook 2 minutes. Remove and peel.

Put cooked pearl onions, sugar, 3/4 cup of the beef stock, and tomato paste into a pan and simmer, covered, until liquid evaporates. Set aside.

Sauté yellow onions, leeks, and shallots in butter and cook slowly 2 minutes. Add pearl onion mixture, 10 cups of beef stock, roasted garlic, and mashed sweet potatoes, and cook 30 minutes. Purée mixture. Return mixture to pan and add white potatoes, carrots, celery, marjoram, savory, and thyme.

Cook mixture 40 minutes. Add reserved half of cooked sweet potato and cook 10 more minutes. Season to taste with salt and pepper.

Each serving provides:

139	Calories	28 g	Carbohydrate
4 g	Protein	187 mg	Sodium
2 g	Fat	7 mg	Cholesterol
3 g	Dietary Fiber		

Herman's Clam Chowder

My Dad is now gone, but we used to love to cook together in the kitchen and make up different recipes. What lovely memories those days are. This is one of his creations (minus the butter). It is not traditional to serve whole clams in their shells in clam chowder, but I just love how it looks—and guests seem to enjoy it.

Makes 8 servings

2	onions, minced
2	teaspoons butter
3/4	teaspoon liquid smoke flavoring
2	tablespoons vermouth
1/4	cup flour
1	cup boiling water
3	cups nonfat milk
1	teaspoon thyme
1	8-ounce bottle clam juice
1/2	cup dry vermouth
3	potatoes, diced small
	salt to taste
2	lemon slices
2	tablespoons Old Bay Seasoning
16	whole clams (optional)
3	cups fresh chopped clams with their juice
1	cup lite evaporated milk
2	tablespoons whiskey
	salt and pepper to taste
	fresh chives for garnish

Put onions and butter into a stock pot and cook until onions are soft. Add smoke flavoring and vermouth. Whisk flour and boiling water together then add to pot. Whisk in milk, thyme, clam juice, vermouth, and potatoes. Cook 20 to 30 minutes, or until potatoes are done. Set aside.

Put some water in a pan and add salt, lemon slices, and Old Bay Seasoning. Bring water to a boil, add optional whole clams, cover, and cook clams in their shells until the shells open, about 5 minutes.

To original soup pot, add fresh, chopped clams and their juice, evaporated milk, whiskey, and salt and pepper to taste. Cook on low simmer for 5 minutes to blend flavors. Stir in clams in their shells.

To serve, fill bowls with soup, put a couple of whole clams in each bowl, snip some chives on top, and serve steaming hot.

Each serving provides:

188	Calories	24 g	Carbohydrate
15 g	Protein	334 mg	Sodium
2 g	Fat	26 mg	Cholesterol
2 g	Dietary Fiber		

Manhattan Clam Chowder

I like to put whole clams in the bowls of soup as a garnish. You can increase the amount of whole clams to suit your fancy.

Makes 10 servings

1	large onion, minced
5	cloves garlic, minced
1	green pepper, diced
5	whole tomatoes, peeled, seeded, and diced
4	cups fish stock (see page 14) or chicken stock, defatted (see page 6)
1	8-ounce bottle clam juice
3/4	teaspoon liquid smoke flavoring
1	11 1/2-ounce can tomato juice
2	cups vermouth
1	teaspoon *each* dried basil, thyme, and marjoram
3	large potatoes, peeled and cut into 1/2-inch dice
1	cup diced carrot
1	cup sliced celery, in 1/2-inch pieces
1/4	cup chopped fresh parsley
1 1/2	pounds fresh clams
10	whole clams in shells
	salt and pepper to taste

Mix onion, garlic, pepper, and tomatoes in a large stock pot and cook 5 minutes. Add fish stock or chicken broth, clam juice, smoke flavoring, tomato juice, vermouth, basil, thyme, marjoram, potatoes, carrots, and celery. Cook for 1 hour. Add parsley, clams, and whole clams, cover, and cook until clams open, 3 to 5 minutes. Taste and season with salt and pepper.

Each serving provides:

194	Calories	19 g	Carbohydrate
23 g	Protein	414 mg	Sodium
2 g	Fat	52 mg	Cholesterol
2 g	Dietary Fiber		

Asparagus and Scallop Chowder

This is so good, just writing down the recipe makes me want to run and get another bowl.

Makes 12 servings

3	leeks, white part only, sliced
5	cloves garlic, minced
2	teaspoons butter
5	cups chicken broth, defatted (see page 6)
2	cups nonfat milk
1/2	cup white wine
2	cups mashed potatoes (mashed with milk, no butter)
1/3	cup fresh, flat-leaf parsley
1	teaspoon dried tarragon
2	bay leaves
3/4	teaspoon liquid smoke flavoring
1	pound tiny red potatoes (peel a little ring around each one)
3/4	cup sliced celery
	hot sauce or tabasco to taste (I like quite a bit)
1	tablespoon fresh lime juice
3/4	pound asparagus, cleaned, peeled, and cut in 1-inch pieces
	salt to taste
1	pound scallops, cut into bite-size pieces

In a large soup pot, sauté the leeks and garlic in butter for 2 minutes. Add the broth, milk, wine, mashed potatoes, parsley, tarragon, bay leaves, smoke flavoring, red potatoes, and celery. Cook mixture, covered, 20 minutes, or until potatoes are tender. Add hot sauce, lime juice, and asparagus and cook 8 more minutes, or until asparagus is done. Discard bay leaves. Season with salt to taste. Add scallops and cook until scallops are done, 2 minutes.

Each serving provides:

136	Calories	20 g	Carbohydrate
11 g	Protein	254 mg	Sodium
1 g	Fat	17 mg	Cholesterol
3 g	Dietary Fiber		

Pepper Chowder

The many varieties of peppers make it fun to experiment.

Makes 12 servings

1	cup minced onion
1	carrot, shredded
3	stalks celery, minced
	vegetable spray
1	green pepper, diced small
1	sweet red pepper, diced small
1	yellow or orange pepper, diced small
1	or 2 small hot peppers, minced
3	cups puréed tomatoes
2	cups cooked black beans
2	cups chicken stock, defatted (see page 6)
1	cup nonfat milk
4	medium potatoes, peeled and diced
1	tablespoon minced fresh cilantro
1	teaspoon dried oregano
1	teaspoon dried basil
	salt and pepper to taste
1	cup lite evaporated milk
2	tablespoons arrowroot mixed with 4 tablespoons water (optional)

Sauté onion, carrot, and celery in a nonstick pan sprayed with vegetable spray. When onion is soft, add peppers, tomatoes, black beans, stock, milk, potatoes, cilantro, oregano, and basil.

Cook on medium heat until potatoes are soft. Add salt and pepper to taste. Stir in evaporated milk. Simmer 3 more minutes. This soup can be thickened with arrowroot mixture.

❖

Each serving provides:

132	Calories	26 g	Carbohydrate
7 g	Protein	190 mg	Sodium
1 g	Fat	2 mg	Cholesterol
4 g	Dietary Fiber		

Cajun Chicken and Shrimp Gumbo

I love hot and spicy food, so this gumbo is one of my favorites. The base for a good gumbo is a nice, dark roux, which is what gives gumbo its wonderful dark color. Roux is usually made by using lots of butter and browning the flour before mixing it into the liquid. To cut the fat I spread flour on a small baking sheet, put it into a 450° oven for 6 to 7 minutes to brown, stirring it once or twice.

Makes 8 servings

4	chicken breast halves, boned, skinned, and cut in half
	vegetable spray
3	tablespoons flour, browned (see above)
3/4	cup boiling water
1	cup minced onion
4	cloves garlic, minced
1/2	cup minced celery
1/2	cup minced carrot
2	cups tomato, peeled and pureed
2	red bell peppers, charred, peeled, seeded, and diced
1/2	teaspoon black pepper
1 1/2	teaspoons cayenne
1	teaspoon dried oregano
1	teaspoon dried basil
2	teaspoons paprika
3	cups chicken stock, defatted (see page 6)
1	8-ounce bottle clam juice
2	cups hot water

1   tablespoon gumbo filé powder
3/4   pound shrimp, peeled and deveined

Sauté chicken breast pieces on high heat, in a nonstick pan with vegetable spray until chicken is browned. Set aside. To make the roux, brown roux as described in recipe introduction. Stir boiling water into browned flour and blend well. Set aside.

Put onion, garlic, celery, carrot, tomato, and peppers into a stock pot and cook together for 15 minutes over low heat. Add black pepper, cayenne, oregano, basil, paprika, chicken stock, clam juice, and hot water. Blend well. Bring mixture to a boil and cook 5 minutes. Reduce heat to medium high. Stir in roux and blend well. Stir in gumbo filé powder. Cook 20 minutes. Add chicken and cook 25 minutes more. Add shrimp and cook until shrimp are pink and done. Serve immediately, alone or over rice.

Each serving provides:

155	Calories	11 g	Carbohydrate
22 g	Protein	198 mg	Sodium
3 g	Fat	102 mg	Cholesterol
2 g	Dietary Fiber		

Crock-pot Adaptation

Complete recipe above through adding the gumbo filé powder. Put mixture into the Crock-pot, reducing liquid by only adding enough water to cover ingredients. Cook 4 to 6 hours on low, or 1 1/2 to 2 hours on high. Add shrimp and cook on high for 15 to 30 minutes more, or until shrimp are done. More liquid can be added at this time if desired.

Crab and Okra Gumbo

Roasted garlic tastes wonderful. Cut the top off a head of garlic and put into a small ovenproof dish. Spray the top of the garlic with a little butter-flavored vegetable spray. Pour 3 tablespoons stock over garlic and cover the dish with foil. Bake in a 300° oven for 1½ hours.

Makes 10 servings

1	head garlic, roasted
1/3	cup flour
1	cup boiling water
1	cup chopped onion
1/2	cup *each* chopped carrot and celery
	vegetable spray
1/2	teaspoon liquid smoke flavoring
2	bay leaves
2	teaspoons dried thyme
3	tablespoons chopped fresh parsley
1	tablespoon paprika
1	red bell pepper, chopped
3	cups sliced okra
2	cups chicken stock, defatted (see page 6)
2	cups fish stock (see page 14)
1	15-ounce can tomatoes, chopped
1/2	teaspoon cayenne
	salt and pepper to taste
2	pounds crab meat
1/2	pound crab legs or crab claws, cut into thirds

Roast garlic as described in recipe introduction.

Brown flour in oven (see Cajun Chicken recipe, page 60). Whisk in boiling water until well blended. Blend in baked garlic and set aside.

Sauté onion, carrot, and celery in vegetable spray and cook until vegetables are limp. Add flour mixture, smoke flavoring, bay leaves, thyme, parsley, paprika, red pepper, okra, stocks, tomatoes, and cayenne. Blend well and cook 1 hour. Discard bay leaves. Season with salt and pepper to taste. Add crab meat and crab legs and cook 20 more minutes.

❖

Each serving provides:

157	Calories	13 g	Carbohydrate
21 g	Protein	479 mg	Sodium
2 g	Fat	92 mg	Cholesterol
2 g	Dietary Fiber		

Crock-pot Adaptation

Roast garlic the night before, squeeze out, and save until ready to use. Follow instructions above until cooking for 1 hour. Instead, put mixture into Crock-pot, cover, and cook on low 8 hours, or on high 4 to 6 hours. Add crab and crab legs and continue to cook 30 minutes more on high.

4

HEARTY
LEGUME
SOUPS

———————————————— ❖ ————————————————

B eans are an all-time favorite food that are low in fat and full of protein. They are an important protein to include in the new pyramid concept of healthy eating. Claims are also being made that beans help fight cholesterol and heart disease.

Few people can resist sitting down to a robust meal made with beans. There are so many ways to use beans; when I go to the local farmers' market I get excited by the wide variety available.

I have always had trouble remembering to pull beans out the night before I am planning to cook with them to soak them for 12 hours. That problem can be solved by putting uncooked beans in a pot and covering them with a gallon of water. Bring to a boil for 10 minutes. Remove pot from stove, cover, and let beans sit 1 hour. Drain and continue with your recipe as if you had soaked the beans overnight.

You can also buy many kinds of canned beans. These are great to use in recipes when you are in a hurry. I usually drain and rinse the beans before I use them, but it is not always necessary. If you use canned beans, be sure to read the labels and be aware of the fat and sodium content.

PEPPERY BEAN MElody

Try this . . . it seems too easy to be so good.

Makes 12 servings

1¹/₂	cups diced onion
2	cloves garlic, minced
1	large green pepper and red pepper, diced
1	cup diced, peeled, and seeded tomato
2	carrots, shredded
1	teaspoon liquid smoke flavoring
1	bay leaf
1¹/₂	teaspoons chili powder
1	tablespoon Worcestershire sauce
¹/₂	cup *each* black beans, white beans, kidney beans, and pinto beans
¹/₂	cup chopped cilantro
4	cups vegetable stock (see page 12)
1	cup strong coffee
4	cups tomato juice
¹/₂	cup tequila
	salt and pepper to taste

Add all ingredients to a soup pot and cook 2 hours. Remove bay leaf and season to taste with salt and pepper.

❖

Each serving provides:

174	Calories	33 g	Carbohydrate
9 g	Protein	318 mg	Sodium
1 g	Fat	0 mg	Cholesterol
5 g	Dietary Fiber		

Smokey Lentil Soup

This delicious, hearty soup is much more delightful to the eyes when made with red or yellow lentils. When I was little I never ate lentil soup; I think it was because I was put off by the grayish brown color.

Makes 8 servings

16	ounces lentils
1	small onion, diced
2	cloves garlic, minced
2	teaspoons olive oil
2	stalks celery, diced small
1/2	teaspoon liquid smoke flavoring
2	bay leaves
6	cups chicken stock, defatted (see page 6)
2	cups water
1	teaspoon cumin
	salt to taste

Sort through lentils and discard discolored ones.

Sauté onion and garlic in olive oil. Add celery, lentils, smoke flavoring, bay leaves, stock, and water and cook until lentils are soft, about 1 to 1 1/2 hours. Add water as needed at any time.

Remove bay leaves and season with cumin. Taste before adding
salt and add if necessary (the smoke flavoring adds a salty
taste).

Each serving provides:

227	Calories	37 g	Carbohydrate
16 g	Protein	161 mg	Sodium
2 g	Fat	2 mg	Cholesterol
8 g	Dietary Fiber		

Crock-pot Adaptation

Follow the recipe until all ingredients go into pan. Instead, put ingredients into Crock-pot, minus 2 cups of the stock. More stock can be
added at end of cooking if necessary. Cook on low 10 to 12 hours, or
on high 5 to 6 hours. Remove bay leaves and season to taste with
cumin and salt.

Black Bean Wonton Soup

These flavorful wontons float in a light, delicious onion broth.

Makes 8 servings

2	cups sliced onion
2	teaspoons butter
1/2	cup plus 2 cups chicken stock, defatted (see page 6)
8	cups water
1 1/2	teaspoons white pepper
	salt to taste
1 1/2	cups cooked black beans
2	green onions, thinly sliced
2	cloves garlic, minced
1/3	cup minced red pepper
1	teaspoon grated fresh ginger
1	tablespoon chopped fresh cilantro
1/4	teaspoon salt
24	wonton wrappers
	fresh cilantro for garnish

Cook onions slowly in butter and 1/2 cup stock until all liquid evaporates. Add water and 2 cups stock, cover, and cook 1 1/2 hours. Strain liquid and discard onions. Taste and season with pepper and salt as needed.

Mash beans slightly. Mix beans, green onions, garlic, pepper, ginger, cilantro, and salt. Spoon a few teaspoons of bean mixture into a wonton wrapper. Wet edges and fold in half over bean mixture. When all done, bring stock to a simmer, add wontons, and cook 5 minutes, or until wontons are done.

Serve a few wontons in each bowl of broth and sprinkle each bowl with a little fresh cilantro.

❖

Each serving provides:

158	Calories	31 g	Carbohydrate
7 g	Protein	264 mg	Sodium
1 g	Fat	4 mg	Cholesterol
3 g	Dietary Fiber		

Navy Bean and Vegetable Soup

For this nutritious soup, you can substitute any vegetables in your garden or refrigerator.

Makes 12 servings

1¹/₂	cups dried navy beans
1	cup chopped onion
4	cloves garlic, minced
¹/₈	to ¹/₄ teaspoon red pepper flakes
	vegetable spray
4	large tomatoes, peeled, seeded, and diced
6	cups beef stock, defatted (see page 10)
3	cups tomato juice
2	carrots, diced
2	stalks celery, diced
2	turnips, peeled and diced
1	cup green beans, cut in ¹/₂-inch lengths
3	zucchini, diced
1¹/₂	cups chopped cabbage
1	teaspoon dried marjoram
¹/₃	cup chopped fresh parsley
1	teaspoon pepper
	salt to taste

Soak beans overnight, or quick soak (see page 66). Sauté onion, garlic, and red pepper flakes in a nonstick stock pot sprayed with vegetable spray. Sauté long and slow. Add tomatoes, stock, tomato juice, and beans and cook 2 hours, or until beans are done. Add carrots, celery, turnips, and green beans and cook 15 minutes more. Add zucchini, cabbage, marjoram, parsley, and pepper and cook 15 minutes more. Season with salt as necessary.

❖

Each serving provides:

135	Calories	25 g	Carbohydrate
8 g	Protein	397 mg	Sodium
1 g	Fat	3 mg	Cholesterol
5 g	Dietary Fiber		

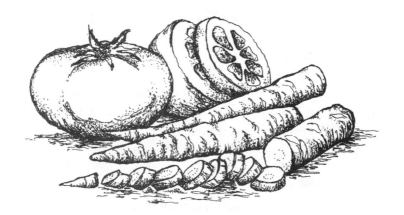

Split Pea and Carrot Soup

This homey soup is so easy to make.

Makes 8 servings

3	leeks, cleaned and chopped
	butter-flavored vegetable spray
1¹/₂	cups split peas
8	cups chicken stock, defatted (see page 6)
2	cups shredded carrots
1	cup peeled and diced potato
¹/₂	teaspoon liquid smoke flavoring
1	tablespoon *each* fresh tarragon and parsley
1	teaspoon white pepper
	salt to taste

Sauté leeks in a nonstick stock pot with butter-flavored vegetable spray for 2 minutes. Add all other ingredients except salt and cook 40 minutes, or until peas and potatoes are done. Purée soup and season with salt as necessary.

❖

Each serving provides:

155	Calories	28 g	Carbohydrate
9 g	Protein	165 mg	Sodium
1 g	Fat	3 mg	Cholesterol
4 g	Dietary Fiber		

Crock-pot Adaptation

Follow recipe until all ingredients are to be put into pot. Instead, put
ingredients into a Crock-pot with just enough liquid to cover them;
add more at the end of cooking if necessary. Cook on low 6 to 7 hours
or on high 3 to 4 hours. Season and purée before serving.

Garbanzo Bean Soup with Cilantro Cream

If you would rather start with uncooked garbanzo beans you can buy them at most farmers' markets.

Makes 12 servings

1/4	cup *each* chopped parsley and cilantro
1/3	cup lite evaporated milk
1/3	cup nonfat sour cream
	salt and pepper to taste
1	large onion, minced
4	cloves garlic, minced
3/4	pound sirloin steak, cubed
2	teaspoons virgin olive oil
3	cups cooked garbanzo beans
1	cup cooked kidney beans
3	whole tomatoes, peeled, seeded, and diced
1	cup diced carrot
1/3	cup chopped cilantro
8	cups chicken stock, defatted (see page 6)
1	11.5-ounce can tomato juice
1/2	teaspoon hot sauce (or to taste)
1	teaspoon cumin
	salt to taste

Mix parsley, 1/4 cup cilantro, evaporated milk, and nonfat sour cream together and season with salt and pepper. Set aside.

Sauté onion, garlic, and steak in olive oil until meat browns slightly. Mash 1 1/2 cups of the garbanzo beans and put into pan with meat. Add remaining garbanzo beans, kidney beans, tomatoes, carrots, 1/3 cup cilantro, stock, tomato juice, hot sauce, and cumin and cook 45 minutes. Add salt to taste.

To serve, ladle into a warm bowl and swirl 1 tablespoon of the cilantro cream mixture set aside earlier into each dish.

❖

Each serving provides:

201	Calories	22 g	Carbohydrate
13 g	Protein	292 mg	Sodium
7 g	Fat	21 mg	Cholesterol
3 g	Dietary Fiber		

VEGETARIAN MEXICAN SOUP

By baking the tortillas, sprayed with a little vegetable spray, they become very crisp. Tortilla strips are also delicious just dipped in salsa.

Makes 8 servings

3	corn tortillas, cut into strips
	vegetable spray
3	mild, long, green chilies, roasted, peeled, and diced
1	large onion, chopped
4	cloves garlic, minced
3	large tomatoes, peeled, seeded, and diced
6	cups vegetable stock (see page 12)
1	30-ounce can lowfat refried beans
1	cup corn kernels
2	zucchini, diced
1	chayote, peeled and diced
1	teaspoon oregano
1/2	teaspoon cayenne
1/3	cup chopped cilantro
	salt to taste
	nonfat sour cream for garnish

Cut tortillas into 1/4-inch strips and put on a cookie sheet. Spray with vegetable spray and cook in a 375° oven until crisp. Set aside.

To roast chili peppers, hold over open flame or put under broiler until blackened. Remove and put into a zipped plastic bag and leave for 3 minutes. Peel and dice.

Sauté onion, garlic, and chilies in vegetable spray, slowly, for

2 minutes. Add tomatoes, vegetable stock, and beans. Blend in beans well. Cook 30 minutes. Purée mixture. Return to pan and add corn, zucchini, chayotes, oregano, cayenne, cilantro, and salt. Cook 15 to 20 minutes more.

To serve, ladle soup into bowls and sprinkle with tortilla strips. Dot with a teaspoon of nonfat sour cream.

❖

Each serving provides:

229	Calories	45 g	Carbohydrate
10 g	Protein	613 mg	Sodium
2 g	Fat	0 mg	Cholesterol
11 g	Dietary Fiber		

Black-Eyed Pea Soup

I love how black-eyed peas look. Besides in soup, I use them in salads, casseroles, or as a beautiful side dish.

Makes 8 servings

1	pound black-eyed peas, picked over and soaked overnight
1	medium onion, chopped
4	cloves garlic, minced
2	red bell peppers, charred and chopped vegetable spray
2	tomatoes, peeled and diced
1/2	cup uncooked rice
2	carrots, shredded
2	whole chicken breasts, boned, skinned, and diced
1/2	teaspoon tabasco sauce
3/4	teaspoon liquid smoke flavoring
8	cups chicken stock, defatted (see page 6)
1/2	cup white wine
1/2	pound chard, stalks diced, leaves slivered
1	teaspoon black pepper
	salt to taste

After soaking overnight, put black-eyed peas in a pan and cover with water. Cover and cook 2 hours. Drain.

Sauté onion, garlic, and charred (see page 39) peppers in vegetable spray until onions are soft. Add black-eyed peas, tomatoes, rice, carrots, chicken, tabasco, smoke flavoring, stock, and wine. Cook 30 minutes. Add chard stalks and cook 10 minutes. Add chard leaves and pepper and cook 5 minutes more. Salt to taste.

Each serving provides:

322	Calories	48 g	Carbohydrate
28 g	Protein	267 mg	Sodium
2 g	Fat	37 mg	Cholesterol
16 g	Dietary Fiber		

White Bean and Spinach Soup

To roast garlic, cut top off 1 head of garlic and put into small oven-proof container (custard cups work well). Spray top with vegetable spray and put 2 tablespoons beef broth into container. Cover tightly with foil and bake in a 300° oven for 1½ hours.

Makes 12 servings

4	leeks, white part only, sliced
1	teaspoon butter
1	head garlic, roasted (see above)
8	cups beef stock, defatted (see page 10)
1	cup red wine
³/₄	teaspoon liquid smoke flavoring
2	cups turkey, cooked and diced
2	bay leaves
½	teaspoon coriander seed, crushed
2	carrots, diced
2	stalks celery, diced
2	tomatoes, peeled, seeded, and diced
2	cups cooked white beans
15	tiny red potatoes, unpeeled and cut in half
1	cup corn kernels
1	pound spinach, chopped
	salt and pepper to taste

Sauté leeks in butter. Mash roasted garlic and add to leeks. Whisk in stock, wine, and smoke flavoring. Add turkey, bay leaves, coriander, carrots, celery, tomatoes, beans, potatoes, and corn. Cook 20 minutes, or until potatoes are tender. Remove bay leaves. Add spinach, and salt and pepper to taste. Cook 10 minutes more.

❖

Each serving provides:

213	Calories	34 g	Carbohydrate
15 g	Protein	255 mg	Sodium
3 g	Fat	23 mg	Cholesterol
7 g	Dietary Fiber		

Green Bean Soup with Sorrel Purée

On busy days, this makes a great quick dinner.

Makes 8 servings

Green bean soup

3	cloves garlic, minced
1	red pepper, minced
2	leeks, white part only, sliced
2	teaspoons unsalted butter
1	carrot, shredded
10	ounces lima beans
9	ounces Italian beans
1	cup fresh green beans, cut in 1/2-inch lengths
2	parsnips, peeled and diced
6	cups chicken stock, defatted (see page 6)
1	teaspoon chicken soup base (or chicken bouillon cube)
1	teaspoon sage
1	teaspoon thyme
	salt and pepper to taste

Sorrel purée

1/4	cup sorrel leaves
1	tablespoon nonfat sour cream
2	teaspoons fat free cream cheese
	salt and pepper to taste
1	tablespoon dry white wine

Sauté the garlic, pepper, and leeks in butter for 2 minutes. Add carrot, beans, parsnips, stock, soup base, sage, and thyme and cook 30 minutes. Season with salt and pepper and serve with a swirl of sorrel purée.

To make sorrel purée: Put sorrel leaves, sour cream, cream cheese, salt, pepper, and wine in a blender and blend well.

Each serving provides:

131	Calories	25 g	Carbohydrate
6 g	Protein	384 mg	Sodium
2 g	Fat	5 mg	Cholesterol
4 g	Dietary Fiber		

Mixed Bean Soup

Served with fresh bread and a salad, this makes for a very sturdy meal.

Makes 8 servings

2	cups onion, chopped
3	cloves garlic, minced
2	teaspoons virgin olive oil
2	cups dried mixed beans, soaked overnight and drained
4	tomatoes, peeled, seeded, and chopped
1	large green pepper, minced
3/4	teaspoon liquid smoke flavoring
1/2	teaspoon cumin
1/4	teaspoon allspice
1	teaspoon coriander
2	carrots, chopped
1/4	cup chopped parsley
4	cups water
4	cups vegetable stock (see page 12)
	salt and pepper to taste

Sauté onion and garlic in olive oil until onion is soft. Add all ingredients except salt and pepper, and let cook 2 hours. Mash the beans a little in the pot and season with salt and pepper.

❖

Each serving provides:

251	Calories	47 g	Carbohydrate
13 g	Protein	156 mg	Sodium
2 g	Fat	0 mg	Cholesterol
8 g	Dietary Fiber		

Pork and Bean Soup with Hominy

Pork tenderloin is a great lean and tender piece of meat to use in low-fat cooking.

Makes 10 servings

3/4	pound pork tenderloin, all fat removed, diced or ground
1	medium onion, minced
4	cloves garlic, minced
	vegetable spray
2	tablespoons white vinegar
1/2	teaspoon liquid smoke flavoring
1	17-ounce can tomato sauce
2	tomatoes, peeled, seeded, and diced
1	15-ounce can hominy
1 1/2	cups pink beans, sorted and soaked overnight
1/4	cup molasses
1	teaspoon chili powder
1	teaspoon coriander
6	cups water

Sauté pork, onion, and garlic in vegetable spray until tenderloin is no longer pink. Add vinegar, smoke flavoring, tomato

sauce, tomatoes, hominy, beans, molasses, chili powder, coriander, and water. Cook mixture 2 hours, or until beans are tender.
Season with salt and pepper.

❖

Each serving provides:

301	Calories	48 g	Carbohydrate
20 g	Protein	496 mg	Sodium
4 g	Fat	23 mg	Cholesterol
7 g	Dietary Fiber		

Crock-pot Adaptation

After soaking beans overnight, drain, cover with fresh water, bring to
a boil for 10 minutes. Drain and then follow instructions until cooking
time. At this time put ingredients into Crock-pot, adding only enough
water to cover ingredients. (If desired, add more liquid at the end of
cooking time.) Cook on high 5 to 6 hours. Season with salt and pepper.

5

Soothing Poultry Soups

A merica's love of chicken is easy to understand. It is nutritious, inexpensive, and the number of flavors it can blend with is virtually limitless.

From the time I was a wee one I have found comfort in chicken soup. Whenever I was feeling bad my mother would fix me some wonderful homemade chicken soup to heal my wounds. I have continued this practice while bringing up my six children.

For hundreds of years chicken soup has been a cure-all for nourishing the body and soul. Every restaurant, in fact every country, has their favorite soup based upon the chicken. This chapter is full of many delightful and gratifying combinations that will sustain us all.

CREAMY TURKEY AND VEGETABLE SOUP

This is a rich and satisfying soup.

Makes 10 servings

2	leeks, thinly sliced
1	pound turkey breast, diced
1/2	cup sliced mushrooms
1/2	cup plus 8 cups chicken stock, defatted (see page 6)
1	cup mashed potato
1	cup broccoli flowerets
1	cup peeled and sliced broccoli stems
1/2	pound green beans, cut into 1-inch pieces
2	carrots, peeled and cut into large dice
3	yellow squash, cut into large dice
1/3	cup chopped fresh parsley
1/2	cup lite evaporated milk
	salt and fresh ground pepper to taste

Put leeks, turkey, and mushrooms with 1/2 cup stock in a non-stick pan and cook until all stock evaporates and meat has begun to cook. Add rest of stock, mashed potato, broccoli buds and stems, green beans, and carrots and cook for 20 minutes. Add squash and parsley and cook 10 minutes more. Stir in evaporated milk, season with salt and pepper, and cook over low heat 5 minutes more. Do not let boil.

❖

Each serving provides:

113	Calories	16 g	Carbohydrate
11 g	Protein	264 mg	Sodium
1 g	Fat	22 mg	Cholesterol
3 g	Dietary Fiber		

Tomato, Chicken, and Rice Soup

Tomato soups are always a welcome sight to my family, but they are especially delicious when tomatoes are at their peak of ripeness.

Makes 8 servings

3	cloves garlic, chopped
1	onion, chopped
2	tomatoes, peeled and diced
3	tomatoes, peeled and puréed
1	tablespoon balsamic vinegar
1 1/2	teaspoons dried thyme
2	tablespoons chopped fresh parsley
3	cups chicken stock, defatted (see page 6)
1	cup nonfat milk
2	whole cooked chicken breasts, boned, skinned, and diced
1/2	cup rice
1 1/2	cups sliced kale
	salt and pepper to taste

In a stock pot, sauté garlic, onion, tomato dice, and tomato purée for 10 minutes. Add vinegar, thyme, parsley, stock, milk, and chicken. Simmer 20 minutes.

Add rice and cook 20 minutes more. Add kale and cook 10 minutes more. Season with salt and pepper to taste.

❖

Each serving provides:

156	Calories	19 g	Carbohydrate
17 g	Protein	76 mg	Sodium
1 g	Fat	36 mg	Cholesterol
2 g	Dietary Fiber		

Chicken and Jalapeño Soup

When making this soup and working with chilies, please take care not to touch your face or eyes. It is also a good idea to wear gloves when working with hot peppers. Peppers can cause severe burning!

Makes 10 servings

1	large onion, chopped
2	cloves garlic, minced
1	jalapeño chili, seeded and minced
	vegetable spray
6	cups chicken stock, defatted (see page 6)
2	large tomatoes, peeled, seeded, and chopped
2	stalks celery, sliced
1	tablespoon lime juice
1	teaspoon dried oregano
1	teaspoon cumin
3	cups diced zucchini or chayote squash
1	12-ounce can whole kernel corn
3	cooked chicken breast halves, boned, skinned, and diced small
3	corn tortillas, sliced into thin strips for garnish
	nonfat sour cream for garnish

Preheat oven to 400°.

Sauté onion, garlic, and jalapeño in a nonstick pan sprayed with vegetable spray until onion becomes soft. Add stock, tomatoes, celery, lime juice, oregano, and cumin, and cook 20 minutes. Add zucchini or chayote and cook 10 minutes more. Purée soup.

Return soup to pan and add corn and chicken. Simmer 15 minutes. Put tortilla chips on a cookie sheet, spray lightly with vegetable spray, and place in a 400° oven until lightly browned.

To serve, top with a dollop of nonfat sour cream and tortilla strips as garnish.

Each serving provides:

122	Calories	16 g	Carbohydrate
11 g	Protein	170 mg	Sodium
2 g	Fat	24 mg	Cholesterol
2 g	Dietary Fiber		

Spicy Chinese Chicken Soup

I like to cook the vegetables and noodles separately for this soup to re-duce cloudiness and distinguish flavors.

Makes 4 servings

bouquet garni:

> 2 green onions, cut in thirds
>
> 3 whole cloves garlic, peeled
>
> 1 inch fresh ginger, peeled
>
> 1 tablespoon fresh coriander

6	cups unsalted chicken stock, defatted (see page 6)
1	teaspoon chili oil
1	tablespoon lite soy sauce
2	tablespoons dry sherry
1	whole chicken breast, boned, skinned, and thinly sliced
6	snow peas, slivered
1	carrot, cut in small dice
1	teaspoon sesame oil
2	green onions, cut diagonally, thinly sliced
$1/2$	cup Chinese egg noodles, cooked

Wrap bouquet garni in cheesecloth and tie. Add bouquet to stock and bring to full boil. Turn heat down and simmer stock 10 minutes. Remove garni and discard. Stir chili oil, soy sauce, and sherry into stock. Set aside.

Cook chicken in boiling water for 10 minutes, or until chicken is done. Remove and drain. Sauté snow peas and carrots in sesame oil 2 minutes.

Bring broth to boil again and add chicken, vegetables, green onions, and noodles. Reduce heat and simmer 5 minutes.

❖

Each serving provides:

198	Calories	18 g	Carbohydrate
18 g	Protein	222 mg	Sodium
5 g	Fat	58 mg	Cholesterol
2 g	Dietary Fiber		

Pilaf and Chicken Soup

To toast almonds, put in a dry, hot, nonstick pan and shake over heat until golden. Remove from pan and set aside.

Makes 8 servings

1	onion, chopped
2	cloves garlic, minced
1½	cups raw rice
1½	ounces vermicelli, broken into ¾-inch pieces
½	cup chopped mushrooms
2	teaspoons unsalted butter
1	carrot, shredded
1	stalk celery, minced
3	chicken breast halves, boned, skinned, and slivered
¼	cup fresh chopped parsley
6	cups chicken stock, defatted (see page 6)
½	cup white wine
	salt and pepper to taste
2	tablespoons toasted, sliced almonds for garnish

Put onion, garlic, rice, vermicelli, and mushrooms in a nonstick stock pot with the butter. Stir and sauté until ingredients begin to brown, about 10 minutes. Add carrot, celery, chicken, parsley, stock, and wine, blending well. Cook mixture 30 minutes. Season with salt and pepper and ladle into bowls. Sprinkle a teaspoon of sliced almonds on each bowl and serve.

Each serving provides:

220	Calories	36 g	Carbohydrate
10 g	Protein	173 mg	Sodium
3 g	Fat	18 mg	Cholesterol
2 g	Dietary Fiber		

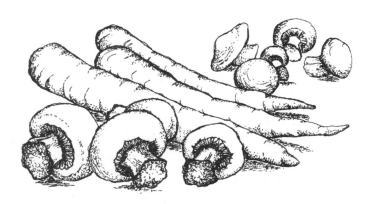

CREAMY ZUCCHINI CHICKEN SOUP

This is a great way to help use up a bumper crop of zucchini.

Makes 10 servings

1	head garlic, roasted
	vegetable spray
6	cups chicken stock, defatted (see page 6)
1/2	cup minced onion
2	cups nonfat milk
2	whole cooked chicken breasts, skinned and diced
1/4	cup chopped fresh parsley
1	teaspoon dried chervil
2	carrots, shredded
2	turnips, cooked and puréed
1/2	cup uncooked elbow macaroni
1	cup sliced zucchini
1	cup lite evaporated milk
2	tablespoons whiskey
	salt and pepper to taste

To roast garlic, cut off top of garlic and put into a small oven-proof bowl. Spray top of garlic with vegetable spray. Spoon 2 tablespoons of the chicken stock over garlic. Cover tightly with foil and cook in a 325° oven for 1 1/2 hours. Mash garlic and set aside.

Sauté onion in 1/4 cup of the chicken stock. Add the rest of the chicken stock and milk and whisk mashed, roasted garlic into mixture. Add chicken, parsley, chervil, carrots, and turnips.

Cook 20 minutes. Add macaroni and zucchini and cook 20 minutes more, or until macaroni is done. Add evaporated milk and whiskey and simmer 2 minutes to blend. Season with salt and pepper to taste.

❖

Each serving provides:

148	Calories	15 g	Carbohydrate
16 g	Protein	246 mg	Sodium
2 g	Fat	33 mg	Cholesterol
1 g	Dietary Fiber		

Ravioli Soup

Homemade raviolis are delicious. But for those who do not want to make their own, wontons work beautifully for this soup.

Makes 8 servings

1/2	cup nonfat cottage cheese
1	zucchini, shredded
1	carrot, shredded
2	large white mushrooms, minced
1	clove garlic, minced
2	tablespoons minced onion
2	teaspoons virgin olive oil
1	teaspoon vegetable seasoning (such as Vegit®)
1/2	teaspoon *each* salt and fresh pepper
1	teaspoon dried basil
2	small cooked chicken breasts, skinned and minced
2	tablespoons grated Parmesan cheese
2	egg whites
2	tablespoons plain breadcrumbs
40	wonton wrappers
8	cups chicken stock, defatted (see page 6)
1/4	cup whole Italian parsley leaves

Put cottage cheese in a small strainer and let sit for 30 minutes.

Sauté zucchini, carrot, mushrooms, garlic, and onion in olive oil, in a nonstick pan that is very hot, until vegetables begin to brown. Remove and let drain in a small strainer for 10 minutes.

In a bowl, mix the cottage cheese, vegetable mixture, vegetable seasoning, salt and pepper, basil, chicken, cheese, egg whites, and breadcrumbs together until well mixed.

Take wonton wrappers and put a heaping teaspoon of the chicken mixture in the center of each one. Wet edges of wonton with water and fold in half. Press to seal well. Continue with wontons until all filling is used.

Heat chicken stock and parsley to a boil. Turn heat down and add wontons. Simmer until wontons are done, about 3 to 5 minutes.

To serve, spoon 5 wontons and ladle some broth into each bowl.

Each serving provides:

332	Calories	53 g	Carbohydrate
23 g	Protein	398 mg	Sodium
3 g	Fat	34 mg	Cholesterol
3 g	Dietary Fiber		

Chicken Dijon with Artichokes and Brandy Soup

Artichokes and chicken are one of my favorite combinations.

Makes 8 servings

1	bunch green onions, sliced
2	whole chicken breasts, boned, skinned, and diced
2	teaspoons unsalted butter
1/3	cup Dijon mustard (smooth type)
2	cups mashed potatoes
1	8 1/2-ounce can artichoke hearts, drained and chopped
3	inner stalks celery, with leaves
1	cup white wine
4	cups chicken stock, defatted (see page 6)
1	tablespoon minced fresh tarragon (1 teaspoon dried)
2	tablespoons chopped fresh parsley
1	cup lite evaporated milk
2	tablespoons nonfat sour cream
1/4	cup good brandy
	salt and pepper to taste
	chopped fresh parsley for garnish

Sauté green onion and diced chicken in butter until chicken is white. Add next 8 ingredients and simmer 40 minutes.

Combine evaporated milk, sour cream, and brandy. Stir into soup and combine well. Barely simmer 2 minutes. Season with salt and pepper and sprinkle with fresh parsley.

❖

Each serving provides:

197	Calories	18 g	Carbohydrate
19 g	Protein	731 mg	Sodium
4 g	Fat	40 mg	Cholesterol
1 g	Dietary Fiber		

Wild Rice, Chicken, and Mushroom Soup

If you cannot find these speciality mushrooms fresh, they are usually available dried. If dried, soak in warm water for 10 minutes first and then slice.

Makes 10 servings

1	cup wild rice
1	small onion, minced
2	cloves garlic, minced
2	scallions, thinly sliced
2	teaspoons virgin olive oil
8	cups chicken stock, defatted (see page 6)
	rind of 1 lemon
	juice of 1 lemon
1½	teaspoons thyme
3	tablespoons chopped parsley
1	carrot, grated
1	large celery stalk, minced
2	whole chicken breasts, boned, skinned, and diced
½	cup sliced chanterelle mushrooms
½	cup sliced porcini mushrooms
1	cup lite evaporated milk
⅓	cup Madeira wine
	salt and white pepper to taste

Rinse rice under water at least 2 times. Drain and set aside.

Sauté onion, garlic, and scallions in olive oil 2 minutes. Add rice and chicken stock and cook 45 minutes. Add lemon rind

and juice, thyme, parsley, carrot, celery, chicken, and mushrooms and cook 40 minutes more. Stir in evaporated milk,
wine, and salt and pepper to taste. Blend well and heat over
low heat 2 minutes, making sure mixture does not boil.

❖

Each serving provides:

166	Calories	19 g	Carbohydrate
16 g	Protein	217 mg	Sodium
2 g	Fat	31 mg	Cholesterol
2 g	Dietary Fiber		

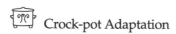
 Crock-pot Adaptation

6

Beefed-Up Soups

—— ❖ ——

When the weather turns cold, is there a better friend than a steaming bowl of rich beef stock that has been simmering for hours? I don't think so.

America is becoming more conscious of fat intake, and thus we tend to eat less beef. Soup is a wonderful way of reducing the amount of beef we use and still getting that satisfying beef flavor.

Spinach and Sirloin Soup

This is a delicious, light beef soup.

Makes 10 servings

2	leeks, white part only, thinly sliced
3/4	pound sirloin, fat removed, and diced
2	cloves garlic, chopped
	vegetable spray
8	cups beef stock, defatted (see page 10)
2	tablespoons minced fresh parsley
4	small celery stalks with leaves attached, sliced
2	carrots, julienned
1	pound spinach, washed, stems removed, and sliced
2	ounces vermicelli
	salt and pepper to taste

Sauté the leeks, sirloin, and garlic in a non-stick pan sprayed with vegetable spray until the sirloin is a little browned. Add beef stock, parsley, celery, and carrots, and cook 40 minutes. Add spinach and vermicelli and cook 15 minutes more. Season with salt and pepper.

Each serving provides:

134	Calories	8 g	Carbohydrate
10 g	Protein	77 mg	Sodium
7 g	Fat	27 mg	Cholesterol
2 g	Dietary Fiber		

Ground Beef and Potato Soup

This soup is reminiscent of a shepherd's pie, but instead of lamb I have chosen to use beef. (Lamb may be used.)

Makes 10 servings

1	cup chopped yellow onion
2	cloves garlic, chopped
	vegetable spray
10	cups beef stock, defatted (see page 10)
1½	pounds potatoes, peeled and diced
1	pound extra-lean ground beef (or lean sirloin you grind)
1	cup peas
1	cup diced carrot
1	cup diced celery
½	cup diced green beans
2	tablespoon chopped fresh parsley
	salt and pepper to taste

Sauté onion and garlic in a nonstick pan sprayed with vegetable spray, until onion is soft. Add stock and potatoes and cook soup until potatoes are soft, about 40 minutes. Purée soup. Blend stock and puréed solids in stock pot.

Sauté ground beef in a nonstick pan until browned. Drain meat and add to soup. Add peas, carrot, celery, beans, and parsley. Cook 20 minutes, or until vegetables are done. Season with salt and pepper. (If you would like to remove more fat from the meat, let soup sit in the refrigerator overnight and remove any fat that accumulates on the top.)

Each serving provides:

187	Calories	18 g	Carbohydrate
14 g	Protein	215 mg	Sodium
7 g	Fat	36 mg	Cholesterol
2 g	Dietary Fiber		

Beef and Green Onion Soup

When you want a fast and easy soup, this is the one.

Makes 8 servings

1	pound lean brisket, cut into 1/2-inch dice
2	bay leaves
2	teaspoons Worcestershire sauce
1/2	teaspoon dried oregano
10	cups beef stock, defatted (see page 10)
1/2	head cabbage, coarsely chopped
1	small red pepper, diced small
4	ounces egg noodles
5	green onions, very thinly sliced, diagonally
	salt and pepper to taste

Put brisket, bay leaves, Worcestershire sauce, oregano, and beef stock into a stock pot. Bring to a boil and skim top of broth. Turn heat down and cook 60 minutes, skimming surface whenever necessary. Remove bay leaves and add cabbage, pepper, and noodles. Cook 10 more minutes. Add green onions, saving a couple of tablespoons for garnish, and cook until noodles and cabbage are done. Season with salt and pepper to taste. Sprinkle with a few green onions and serve.

❖

Each serving provides:

124	Calories	16 g	Carbohydrate
9 g	Protein	63 mg	Sodium
3 g	Fat	31 mg	Cholesterol
2 g	Dietary Fiber		

Tortellini Soup

If you look at the fresh pastas in your supermarket you will be able to find low-fat tortellini.

Makes 8 servings

1	onion, chopped
8	ounces fresh mushrooms, sliced
2	teaspoon virgin olive oil
1	teaspoon white pepper
3	tablespoons flour
1½	cups milk
1½	cups beef stock, defatted (see page 10)
½	cup white wine
1	teaspoon dried thyme
½	teaspoon oregano
1	teaspoon beef soup base
½	cup diced celery
½	cup diced carrot
9	ounces fresh tortellini
	salt and pepper to taste
2	tablespoons nonfat sour cream for garnish
2	tablespoons Parmesan cheese for garnish

Slowly sauté the onion and mushrooms in olive oil for 10 minutes. Sprinkle with white pepper. Add flour and blend until no more flour shows. Whisk in milk. When well blended, add stock, wine, thyme, oregano, soup base, celery, and carrot, and cook 30 minutes. Add tortellini and cook 15 minutes more, or until tortellini is done. Season to taste with salt and pepper. Stir in sour cream and Parmesan cheese, mix well, and serve.

❖

Each serving provides:

181	Calories	11 g	Carbohydrate
9 g	Protein	389 mg	Sodium
6 g	Fat	24 mg	Cholesterol
1 g	Dietary Fiber		

Barley, Veal, and Zucchini Soup

This soup will certainly chase away the winter blues!

Makes 10 servings

1/2	cup pearl barley
1 1/4	cups beef stock, defatted (see page 10)
3	leeks, white part only, sliced
2	cloves garlic, chopped
1	pound veal, cut into little dice
	vegetable spray
1/2	cup celery leaves
1	cup diced carrot
1/2	teaspoon dried thyme
2	bay leaves
2	tablespoons chopped parsley
2	cups diced zucchini
1/4	cup vermouth
	salt and pepper to taste

Put barley and 1 1/4 cups of beef stock into a pan and cook until barley is almost done, about 30 to 40 minutes.

Sauté leeks, garlic, and veal in a pan sprayed with vegetable spray until meat turns color. Add barley, celery leaves, carrot, thyme, bay leaves, parsley, and rest of beef stock. Cook mixture

20 minutes. Add zucchini and vermouth and cook 10 minutes more, or until zucchini is done. Remove bay leaves and season with salt and pepper.

Each serving provides:

138	Calories	8 g	Carbohydrate
17 g	Protein	207 mg	Sodium
4 g	Fat	32 mg	Cholesterol
2 g	Dietary Fiber		

Oxtail Soup

"Oxtails"—the name is a little scary, but they are delicious. Just don't tell your guests what they are.

Makes 8 servings

2 1/2	pounds oxtails, cut into 1 1/2 inch lengths, all fat removed, sprinkled with pepper
2	teaspoons unsalted butter
	vegetable spray
1	cup chopped onion
3	cloves garlic, minced
3	carrots, sliced
2	cups chopped tomatoes
1	bay leaf
1 1/2	teaspoons thyme
1/4	cup chopped parsley
2	cups beer
6	cups beef stock, defatted (see page 10)
	salt and pepper to taste
	chopped, fresh parsley for garnish

Preheat oven to 325°.

Sprinkle oxtails with pepper and brown in hot, ovenproof pan with butter. Remove oxtails, spray pan with vegetable spray, and sauté onions and garlic 2 minutes. Add carrots, tomatoes, bay leaf, thyme, parsley, beer, and beef stock to onion. Return oxtails to pan and cook all ingredients for 3 hours. Add more stock if necessary. Remove bay leaf. Add salt and pepper to taste and sprinkle with fresh parsley.

❖

Each serving provides:

138	Calories	8 g	Carbohydrate
17 g	Protein	207 mg	Sodium
4 g	Fat	32 mg	Cholesterol
2 g	Dietary Fiber		

Crock-pot Adaptation

Follow the instructions until ingredients go into oven. Instead, put all ingredients into Crock-pot and add only enough beef stock to cover ingredients. Cook on high 4 to 6 hours. Season with salt, pepper, and parsley before serving. Add more stock at the end if necessary.

The Best
Vegetable-Beef Soup

Cooking the onion and stock so long makes a savory broth.

Makes 12 servings

2	cups chopped onion
10	cups beef stock, defatted (see page 10)
1	pound sirloin, fat removed and diced
1	cup peeled and sliced broccoli stems
3	celery stalks, chopped, with leaves attached
4	carrots, sliced
3	small crookneck squash, diced
3	small parsnips, peeled and diced
2	small turnips, peeled and diced
1	cup fava beans
2	tomatoes, peeled, seeded, and diced
1	cup peas
1	teaspoon *each* dried basil, tarragon, and savory
1¹/₂	teaspoons fresh pepper
	salt to taste

Put onion and stock in a soup pot. Cook 2 hours. Add sirloin and cook 30 minutes more. Skim top of soup. Add all other ingredients and cook 40 minutes more.

Each serving provides:

224	Calories	27 g	Carbohydrate
13 g	Protein	349 mg	Sodium
8 g	Fat	30 mg	Cholesterol
7 g	Dietary Fiber		

7

Soups from the Sea

My family loves soups from the sea. With the infinite variety of fish available to us today, who couldn't find something they love? Seafood combines beautifully with so many ingredients that you can please everyone.

We spend part of each summer in a quaint, adorable house in Carmel, California. Summers there have many overcast days; coming from the Sacramento area we are delighted with this change in weather. One of the advantages of being in Carmel is the abundance of fresh produce and seafood that is available. I love to indulge in seafood, garlic, luscious fruit, and artichokes while I am there. We go to the wharf in Monterey and get wonderful, fresh fish to make our favorite bouillabaisse, cioppino, chowder, bisque, or whatever other fish soup I feel like conjuring up. The beauty and culinary experience of cooking with great fresh ingredients is available around the world; I am sure we all have our favorite spots.

When buying fresh fish look for bright colored fish that has a sweet, not fishy smell. If possible it is best to buy a whole fish, then cut it up and store what you don't use. When buying a whole fish look for slightly bulging eyes and brightly colored gills. If buying steaks or fillets look for firm, moist fish. Don't buy fish that is off color or brown on the edges.

Most of the shrimp available today has been previously frozen. For this reason I buy my shrimp frozen. If you buy defrosted shrimp make sure they feel firm and are shiny.

When selecting mussels, clams, or oysters in their shells, make sure they are alive and the shells are closed tightly or that they respond quickly when touched.

A Beautiful Bouillabaisse

Be sure to make plenty of this lovely soup so you can share it with friends. The distinct, succulent aroma will dazzle your guests.

Makes 12 servings

1	onion, chopped
3	leeks, white part only, sliced
3	cloves garlic, minced
	olive oil spray
6	tomatoes, peeled and finely chopped
1	red pepper, charred and minced (see page 39)
1	fennel bulb, minced
1	bay leaf
4	cups fish stock (see page 14) or clam juice
2	cups tomato juice
2	cups dry white wine
2	tablespoons chopped fresh Chinese basil (or sweet basil)
2	tablespoons chopped fresh parsley
1	teaspoon dried thyme
1/2	teaspoon saffron
	salt and pepper to taste
3/4	pound lobster meat, cut into bite-size pieces
10	clams or mussels (or a combination of both)
1	pound firm white fish (such as cod, halibut, sea bass), cut into 1-inch pieces
1	pound shrimp, peeled and deveined
3	crab legs, cut into thirds

Sauté onion, leek, and garlic in a nonstick stock pot sprayed with olive oil spray until onion is soft. Add tomatoes, charred peppers, and fennel to pan and continue to sauté for 2 minutes. Add bay leaf, fish stock, tomato juice, wine, basil, parsley, thyme, and saffron and cook mixture 30 minutes. Season with salt and pepper to taste.

Add lobster and clams and cook 10 minutes. Add white fish and cook 2 minutes. Add shrimp, crab, and mussels (if using) and cook until shrimp turn pink and mussels and clams are all the way open, about 5 minutes more. Remove bay leaf and discard.

❖

Each serving provides:

160	Calories	9 g	Carbohydrate
23 g	Protein	515 mg	Sodium
2 g	Fat	90 mg	Cholesterol
2 g	Dietary Fiber		

Favorites-From-the-Sea Cioppino

I named this "Favorites-From-the-Sea" because once you make the delicious broth you can add your favorite seafood. This particular one was my Dad's favorite. After serving this cioppino, save any leftover broth to put on pasta the next day—it is scrumptious.

Makes 8 servings

3	cups chopped onion
3	cloves garlic, chopped
2	bell peppers, chopped
2	stalks celery, chopped
	olive oil spray
	juice of 1 lemon
2	quarts tomatoes, puréed
1	can tomato paste
2	8-ounce bottles clam juice
1	bottle vermouth (fifth) (yes, 1 bottle!!)
1	tablespoon chopped fresh basil
2	tablespoons chopped fresh parsley
1	teaspoon dried oregano
1/2	teaspoon dried thyme
1/2	to 1 teaspoon cayenne
1	tablespoon Worcestershire sauce
2	teaspoons dried Italian seasoning
2	6 1/2-ounce cans minced clams in their juice
2	pounds of white fish (cod, bass, halibut)
16	fresh clams

$^3/_4$ pound shrimp, shelled and deveined
$^1/_2$ pound scallops
4   crab legs, cut in thirds
         salt and pepper to taste

Sauté the onion, garlic, peppers, and celery in a nonstick pan
sprayed with olive oil spray until vegetables begin to soften.
Squeeze lemon juice on vegetables. Add tomatoes, tomato
paste, clam juice, vermouth, basil, parsley, oregano, thyme,
cayenne, Worcestershire sauce, and Italian seasoning and cook
2 hours. Add clams in their juice and cook 30 minutes more.
Add white fish and cook 10 minutes. Add fresh clams and cook
5 minutes more. Add shrimp, scallops, and crab legs and cook
until shrimp are pink and done, and clam shells are open.

Each serving provides:

351	Calories	26 g	Carbohydrate
50 g	Protein	555 mg	Sodium
4 g	Fat	147 mg	Cholesterol
5 g	Dietary Fiber		

Italian White Fish Soup

This is a terrific, hassle-free dish to make for company. You can even make it the day before—just add the fish right before serving.

Makes 10 servings

1	large onion, chopped
6	cloves garlic, chopped
1/2	teaspoon dried red pepper flakes
1/2	cup chopped celery
1	cup sliced mushrooms
	olive oil spray
	juice of 1 lemon
4	cups peeled and crushed tomatoes
4	cups chicken stock, defatted (see page 6)
1	cup fish stock (see page 14) or clam juice
1/2	cup red wine
2	tablespoons chopped fresh basil
1	tablespoon chopped fresh parsley
1/2	teaspoon dried marjoram
1	teaspoon fresh ground pepper
	salt to taste
2	pounds white fish (cod, halibut, bass, snapper, orange roughy), cut into 1-inch squares
	grated Asiago cheese for garnish

Sauté onion, garlic, red pepper flakes, celery, and mushrooms in a nonstick pan sprayed with olive oil spray until onions soften. Squeeze lemon juice on vegetables.

Add tomatoes, chicken stock, fish stock, wine, basil, parsley, marjoram, and pepper to vegetables. Cook soup 30 minutes. Add fish, salt to taste, and cook until fish is done, about 10 minutes. Serve each bowl garnished with a teaspoon of grated Asiago cheese.

❖

Each serving provides:

115	Calories	7 g	Carbohydrate
18 g	Protein	206 mg	Sodium
1 g	Fat	41 mg	Cholesterol
1 g	Dietary Fiber		

Spanish Rice Soup

If you don't like mussels, you can use clams—or just the shrimp.

Makes 10 servings

1	medium onion, diced
3	cloves garlic, minced
1	red bell pepper, diced
1	green bell pepper, diced
	vegetable spray
2	tomatoes, peeled, seeded, and diced
1/2	cup uncooked rice
2	tablespoons lime juice
1/4	cup chopped fresh coriander
1	teaspoon cayenne
1	tablespoon paprika
1	8-ounce bottle clam juice
1/2	cup Rojo (red Spanish wine)
6	cups chicken stock, defatted (see page 6)
	salt and pepper to taste
1	teaspoon saffron
1/2	pound shrimp, peeled and diced
3/4	pound mussels in shells
	chopped, fresh parsley for garnish

Sauté onion, garlic, and peppers in vegetable spray until onion is soft. Add tomatoes, rice, lime juice, coriander, cayenne, paprika, clam juice, wine, and chicken stock. Cook 30 minutes.

Taste for seasoning and add salt and pepper to taste. Add saffron, shrimp, and mussels and cook until mussel shells open and shrimp are pink. Garnish with fresh parsley.

❖

Each serving provides:

116	Calories	14 g	Carbohydrate
10 g	Protein	290 mg	Sodium
2 g	Fat	39 mg	Cholesterol
1 g	Dietary Fiber		

Mediterranean Soup

Fennel adds a nice touch to this delicious fish soup.

Makes 12 servings

3/4	cup onion, minced
2	leeks, white part only, sliced
2	tomatoes, peeled, seeded, and chopped
1	large fennel bulb, diced
2	teaspoons unsalted butter
2	cups cooked chickpeas (garbanzo beans)
2	carrots, thinly sliced
2	zucchini, thinly sliced
1/4	cup chopped Italian parsley
1/4	cup chopped fresh basil
1	cup tomato juice
5	cups chicken stock, defatted (see page 6)
2	ounces dry elbow macaroni
3/4	pound white fish (sea bass, cod, orange roughy), cut into 1-inch pieces
	salt and pepper to taste
	grated Asiago cheese for garnish

Put onion, leeks, tomatoes, fennel, and butter into a stock pot and simmer 10 minutes. Add chickpeas, carrots, zucchini, parsley, basil, tomato juice, and stock and cook 20 minutes. Add macaroni and cook 15 minutes. Add fish and cook 5 minutes more. Season with salt and pepper to taste and garnish with grated Asiago cheese.

Each serving provides:

130	Calories	17 g	Carbohydrate
10 g	Protein	266 mg	Sodium
3 g	Fat	18 mg	Cholesterol
3 g	Dietary Fiber		

Scallop Soup with Saffron

Saffron is expensive, but I love it. It adds a special touch to this soup.

Makes 6 servings

4	leeks, white part only, sliced
2	cloves garlic, crushed
2	teaspoons butter
3	cups fish stock (see page 14)
1	cup chicken stock, defatted (see page 6)
1	cup white wine
1/3	cup minced celery
1/3	cup minced carrot
1/4	cup chopped fresh coriander
1	teaspoon dried thyme
1 1/2	cups cooked peas, puréed
1	teaspoon saffron
	salt and pepper to taste
1/3	cup chopped green onion
1 1/2	pounds scallops, cut into bite-size pieces
1/2	cup evaporated milk
1	to 2 tablespoons brandy
	fresh coriander for garnish

Sauté leeks and garlic in butter until leeks are soft. Add fish stock, chicken stock, wine, celery, carrots, coriander, thyme, peas, and saffron. Cook 20 minutes. Season mixture with salt and pepper to taste. Add green onion and scallops and cook 2 minutes. Stir in evaporated milk and brandy; warm and blend but do not let boil. Garnish with fresh coriander.

Each serving provides:

217	Calories	19 g	Carbohydrate
25 g	Protein	376 mg	Sodium
4 g	Fat	48 mg	Cholesterol
5 g	Dietary Fiber		

8

Garden-Fresh Vegetable Soups

I love vegetable soups all year round, but I especially love them in the summer when my garden is overflowing. I don't think there is anything more satisfying than being able to go in your own back yard and harvest a bounty of colorful vegetables.

Another thing I love to do all year round is go to the local farmers' markets and get different, intriguing items. Here in Sacramento we have a wonderful farmers' market downtown under a freeway. It is full of luscious fruit, vegetables, live fish, breads, flowers, and a wide variety of hard-to-find Asian vegetables and herbs.

When making vegetable soups, be inventive and use some of the vegetables you have noticed in your supermarket but were never brave enough to try. You may be surprised at how well they blend with more familiar ingredients.

Chard, Turnip, and Leek Soup

This soup also looks elegant puréed and topped with a dab of nonfat sour cream.

Makes 6 servings

1	pound swiss chard
1	cup chopped leeks, white part only
2	cloves garlic, minced
1/2	cup plus 3 1/2 cups vegetable stock (see page 12)
2	cups chicken stock, defatted (see page 6)
2	potatoes, peeled and diced
3	turnips, peeled and diced
1	carrot, shredded
1	teaspoon *each* celery seed and dill seed
	fresh ground pepper and salt to taste

Wash chard and separate the leaves and ribs. String the ribs and dice them up. Set aside.

Sauté leeks and garlic in 1/2 cup vegetable stock until stock evaporates. Add the other 3 1/2 cups of vegetable stock, chicken stock, potatoes, turnips, carrot, celery seed, dill seed, and diced chard stems and cook 25 minutes. Add leaves of chard and salt and pepper to taste and cook 5 more minutes.

Each serving provides:

120	Calories	27 g	Carbohydrate
4 g	Protein	347 mg	Sodium
1 g	Fat	1 mg	Cholesterol
3 g	Dietary Fiber		

Tomato Soup with Wild Mushrooms

This soup has a marvelous woodsy flavor due to the delicious wild mushrooms. We are so fortunate with the selection of wild mushrooms that are available in our supermarkets today. These mushrooms are very sandy, so rinse quickly and pat dry so they do not retain too much moisture.

Makes 6 servings

2	leeks, white part only, sliced
1	medium onion, chopped
2	cloves garlic, minced
2	teaspoons unsalted butter
2	tablespoons flour
2	cups chicken stock, defatted (see page 6)
6	large tomatoes, peeled, seeded, and chopped
6	ounces *each* fresh chanterelle mushrooms and fresh shiitake mushrooms, stems removed and diced
1/3	cup chopped fresh parsley
1/4	cup chopped fresh basil
1/2	teaspoon sugar
1/2	cup Madeira wine
	salt and fresh ground pepper to taste

Sauté leeks, onion, and garlic in butter until onion is transparent. Stir in flour until no white from the flour shows. Whisk in the stock and blend well. Add all other ingredients and cook 40 minutes.

❖

Each serving provides:

96	Calories	17 g	Carbohydrate
3 g	Protein	159 mg	Sodium
2 g	Fat	5 mg	Cholesterol
3 g	Dietary Fiber		

Asparagus and Pasta Soup

Here in Granite Bay we have the most beautiful asparagus, grown in the nearby San Joaquin Valley.

Makes 12 servings

4	leeks, white part only, sliced
2	teaspoons unsalted butter
5	cups diced asparagus
1	large red bell pepper, diced
1	large green bell pepper, diced
1	large russet potato, peeled and shredded
8	cups chicken stock, defatted (see page 6)
1/2	cup white wine
1/4	cup chopped fresh basil
1	teaspoon dried chervil
1	teaspoon white pepper
1/2	pound mushrooms, sliced
	butter-flavored vegetable spray
1	carrot, shredded
1 1/2	cup small shell noodles
	salt to taste

Sauté leeks in butter until leeks are limp. Add 3 cups of the asparagus, peppers, potato, stock, wine, basil, chervil, and pepper. Cook mixture 30 minutes. Purée mixture.

In same stock pot, sauté mushrooms in butter flavored vegetable spray. Return puréed soup to pan with mushrooms and add carrots and noodles. Cook soup another 15 minutes or until noodles and asparagus are done. Season with salt to taste.

❖

Each serving provides:

71	Calories	12 g	Carbohydrate
4 g	Protein	159 mg	Sodium
2 g	Fat	4 mg	Cholesterol
2 g	Dietary Fiber		

Jerusalem Artichoke Soup with Asparagus

Jerusalem artichokes are really an ugly vegetable, but don't let this discourage you from using them, for they are very good for your health. Served raw, they have a crunchy texture and taste like water chestnuts. Cooked, their texture is similar to a potato—with a slightly sweet taste.

Makes 8 servings

1	large onion, diced
2	cloves garlic, minced
	butter-flavored vegetable spray
6	cups chicken stock, defatted (see page 6)
1/2	cup vermouth
1	tablespoon Worcestershire sauce
3	carrots, peeled and diced
2	tomatoes, peeled, seeded, and diced
1/2	to 1 teaspoon hot sauce (to taste)
1/4	cup chopped fresh parsley
1/2	teaspoon dried rosemary
1	teaspoon dried thyme
3	cups diced asparagus
1 1/2	cups peeled and diced Jerusalem artichokes
1	cup peas
	salt and pepper to taste

Sauté onion and garlic in a pan with vegetable spray. Add chicken stock, vermouth, Worcestershire sauce, carrots, tomatoes, hot sauce, parsley, rosemary, and thyme to onion mixture and cook 20 minutes to blend flavors. Add asparagus and cook 10 minutes more. Add Jerusalem artichokes and peas and cook 10 minutes more. Season with salt and pepper to taste.

❖

Each serving provides:

146	Calories	30 g	Carbohydrate
5 g	Protein	302 mg	Sodium
1 g	Fat	2 mg	Cholesterol
4 g	Dietary Fiber		

Bourbon Flavored Pumpkin Soup

It wouldn't be Halloween without pumpkin soup served out of a baked pumpkin. Buy one extra little pumpkin, clean it out, and sprinkle the inside with sugar. Put the top of the pumpkin back on and place it on a cookie sheet. Bake in a 350° oven 30 to 40 minutes, depending on the size of pumpkin. Remove from oven and use it as a bowl to serve soup.

Makes 8 servings

1	4-pound pumpkin
4	leeks, white part only, sliced
1	small onion, chopped
2	teaspoons unsalted butter
1	tablespoon sugar
2	tablespoons flour
2	cups orange juice
1	tablespoon orange rind, grated
1	cup diced carrot
1/2	cup diced celery
1	cinnamon stick
2	cups vegetable stock (see page 12)
1	cup lite evaporated milk
2	tablespoons bourbon
	salt and fresh ground pepper to taste

Before creating soup bowl, remove flesh and seeds from pumpkin and cut pumpkin meat into chunks. Sauté leeks and onion in butter until onion turns transparent. Sprinkle onion mixture with sugar and cook 2 minutes more. Stir in flour and blend

❖

until no white from flour shows. Whisk in orange juice. When
blended, add pumpkin, orange rind, carrot, celery, cinnamon
stick, and stock. Cook mixture 40 minutes. Remove cinnamon
stick. Purée soup and return to pan. Add evaporated milk,
bourbon, salt and pepper to taste. Heat over very low heat until
flavors are blended, about 1 minute. Serve in pumpkin bowl.

❖

Each serving provides:

123	Calories	23 g	Carbohydrate
4 g	Protein	187 mg	Sodium
1 g	Fat	4 mg	Cholesterol
2 g	Dietary Fiber		

Old-Fashioned Cream of Tomato Soup with Tarragon

When tomatoes are fresh, this soup can't be beat. Try serving this with croutons made from diced sourdough bread that has been sprayed with butter-flavored vegetable spray and toasted in the oven.

Makes 4 servings

2	leeks, white part only, sliced
1	clove garlic, minced
	good pinch of red pepper flakes (or to taste)
2	teaspoons unsalted butter
2	tablespoons flour
3	cups peeled, seeded, and chopped fresh tomatoes
1	tablespoon chopped fresh tarragon
1/2	cup milk
1/2	cup white wine
1	teaspoon chicken soup base (or bouillon)
1/2	teaspoon sugar
1	cup lite evaporated milk
	salt and pepper to taste

Sauté leeks, garlic, and red pepper flakes in butter for 5 minutes. Stir in flour and blend. Add tomatoes, tarragon, milk, wine, soup base, and sugar; blend well and cook 15 minutes.

❖

Purée soup in a blender or food processor. Put soup back into soup pan, stir in evaporated milk, and season to taste with salt and pepper. Warm gently until hot.

❖

Each serving provides:

148	Calories	20 g	Carbohydrate
8 g	Protein	361 mg	Sodium
4 g	Fat	12 mg	Cholesterol
2 g	Dietary Fiber		

CREAMY BROCCOLI
SOUP WITH PESTO

A little swirl of pesto in this soup is absolutely heavenly for those of us cutting our fat, but still yearning for the wonderful flavor of pesto.

Makes 12 servings

Broccoli soup

3	leeks, white part only, sliced
2	teaspoons unsalted butter
3	tablespoons flour
1	cup nonfat milk
2	zucchini, thinly sliced
1/2	cup thinly sliced celery
2	carrots, peeled and thinly sliced
2	cups broccoli flowerets
8	ounces white mushrooms, thinly sliced
1	teaspoon chervil
1	teaspoon thyme
6	cups chicken stock, defatted (see page 6)
1	cup lite evaporated milk
	salt and pepper to taste

Pesto

1/4	cup celery leaves
1/4	cup fresh basil
2	cloves garlic
1	tablespoon Parmesan cheese

2   teaspoons virgin olive oil
2   teaspoons pinenuts (optional)
         salt and pepper to taste

Sauté leeks in butter for 2 minutes. Add flour and blend. Whisk
in milk until flour is blended. Add zucchini, celery, carrots,
broccoli, mushrooms, chervil, thyme, and stock. Simmer 45
minutes. Stir in evaporated milk and season with salt and pepper. Ladle into dish and put a teaspoon of pesto into each
bowl.

To make pesto: Put celery leaves, basil, and garlic into a
blender or processor. Swirl a few times. Add cheese, oil, and
pinenuts (if desired), and season with salt and pepper to taste.
Makes about 1/3 cup.

Each serving provides:

78	Calories	11 g	Carbohydrate
5 g	Protein	335 mg	Sodium
2 g	Fat	5 mg	Cholesterol
2 g	Dietary Fiber		

FAVORITE MINESTRONE

Roasted garlic stirred into the stock of a soup gives an intriguing and exotic flavor. This is not a real thick minestrone; it is light and fresh tasting.

Makes 10 servings

1	head garlic, roasted
2	cups chopped onion
	vegetable spray
10	cups vegetable stock (see page 12)
1/2	cup navy beans, picked over and soaked overnight
2	tomatoes, peeled and finely chopped
1	teaspoon *each* marjoram, oregano, basil
1/4	cup chopped fresh parsley
1	carrot, julienned
1	stalk celery, julienned
1	small zucchini, julienned
1	parsnip, julienned
2	ounces linguine, broken into 2-inch pieces
	salt and pepper to taste
	fresh grated Parmesan cheese for garnish

Preheat oven to 325°.

To roast garlic, cut the top part of the garlic off to expose the cloves. Put into a small ovenproof container (custard cups work well). Put 2 to 3 tablespoons of the vegetable stock into the container with the whole garlic and cover tightly with foil. Put into preheated oven for 1 1/2 hours. Remove and squeeze the garlic into a small dish. Smash garlic and set aside.

Sauté onion in a nonstick pan sprayed with vegetable spray until onion is transparent. Add rest of vegetable stock and roasted garlic, being sure to blend in the garlic well. Add beans, tomatoes, marjoram, oregano, basil, and parsley. Cook 1 1/2 hours. Add vegetables and cook 15 minutes more. Add linguine and cook about 8 minutes more, or until linguine is done. Season to taste with salt and pepper. Sprinkle each dish with a little freshly grated Parmesan cheese.

❖

Each serving provides:

136	Calories	27 g	Carbohydrate
6 g	Protein	182 mg	Sodium
1 g	Fat	1 mg	Cholesterol
3 g	Dietary Fiber		

Citrus Pumpkin Soup

Pumpkin makes a beautiful, autumn colored soup.

Makes 6 servings

1	cup chopped onion
1	cup orange juice
1	teaspoon brown sugar
3	cups pumpkin purée
2½	cups chicken stock, defatted (see page 6)
½	cup lemon juice
1	teaspoon minced lemongrass
2	tablespoons Grand Marnier
2	tablespoons grated lemon rind
½	teaspoon mace
¼	teaspoon nutmeg
1	cup lite evaporated milk
¼	teaspoon white pepper
	salt to taste

Sauté onion, orange juice, and brown sugar together until the juice almost evaporates and the onion browns slightly. Stir in pumpkin, stock, lemon juice, lemongrass, Grand Marnier, lemon rind, mace, and nutmeg and cook for 30 minutes. Stir in evaporated milk, pepper, and salt to taste, and simmer 3 minutes more.

❖

Each serving provides:

124	Calories	25 g	Carbohydrate
6 g	Protein	197 mg	Sodium
1 g	Fat	3 mg	Cholesterol
3 g	Dietary Fiber		

CREAMY CABBAGE SOUP

This is a soothing, creamy soup that my children love.

Makes 8 servings

2	cups shredded green cabbage
3	large potatoes, peeled and diced
1	large onion, chopped
3	cloves garlic, minced
8	cups chicken stock, defatted (see page 6)
1/4	teaspoon liquid smoke flavoring
3	ounces shell noodles
1/2	cup diced mushrooms
2	carrots, very thinly sliced
2	tablespoons chopped fresh parsley
1	teaspoon dried thyme
1 1/2	cups chopped cabbage
1/2	cup lite evaporated milk
	salt and fresh ground pepper to taste

Put shredded cabbage, potatoes, onion, garlic, stock, and smoke flavoring into a stock pot and cook for 40 minutes. Purée solid ingredients then blend stock back into purée.

Add noodles, mushrooms, carrots, parsley, thyme, and chopped cabbage and cook 10 to 15 minutes, or until noodles are done. Stir in evaporated milk and season with salt and pepper. Simmer 3 minutes.

Each serving provides:

130	Calories	26 g	Carbohydrate
6 g	Protein	189 mg	Sodium
1 g	Fat	4 mg	Cholesterol
3 g	Dietary Fiber		

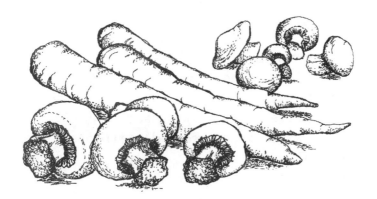

Green Bean, Corn, and Pepper Soup

This colorful and spicy soup can be made with fresh, frozen, or canned whole corn kernels. Vegit® seasoning is a spice found in the health foods department of most large grocery stores.

Makes 12 servings

1/2	cup chopped onion
3	green onions, thinly sliced
4	cloves garlic, minced
2	whole tomatoes, peeled and chopped
1/2	cup tomato juice
8	cups vegetable stock (see page 12)
1	cup dry white wine
1	tablespoon *each* chopped fresh basil, tarragon, and parsley
1	teaspoon vegetable seasoning (such as Vegit®)
1/2	cup *each* diced yellow, red, and green pepper
1 1/2	cups whole corn kernels
1 1/2	cups diced, fresh green beans
4	ounces vermicelli
	several drops of tabasco (to taste)
	salt and fresh ground pepper to taste

Put onion, green onions, garlic, tomatoes, tomato juice, vegetable stock, wine, herbs, and vegetable seasoning into a stock pan and cook 45 minutes. Add peppers, corn, and green beans and cook 20 minutes more. Add vermicelli, tabasco, salt and pepper. Cook until vermicelli is done.

Each serving provides:

103	Calories	22 g	Carbohydrate
3 g	Protein	144 mg	Sodium
1 g	Fat	0 mg	Cholesterol
2 g	Dietary Fiber		

Ravishing Radish Soup

Many people miss out on the delights of radishes. Try them in stir-fries also—they are surprisingly good.

Makes 6 servings

2	shallots, minced
2	green onions, minced
2	cloves garlic, minced
3/4	cup sherry
3	cups vegetable stock (see page 12)
2	cups nonfat milk
3	cups sliced radishes
2	potatoes, diced
2	large fennel bulbs, diced
1	tablespoon fresh tarragon
1¹/₂	teaspoons celery seed
	salt and pepper to taste
1	cup whole watercress leaves
¹/₂	cup lite evaporated milk

Put shallots, green onions, garlic, and sherry into a pan. Cook, reducing liquid to ¹/₄ cup. Add vegetable stock, milk, radishes, potatoes, fennel, tarragon, and celery seed. Cook 20 minutes. Purée mixture.

Season with salt and pepper and add watercress. Cook 5 minutes. Stir in evaporated milk. Heat, but do not let soup boil, for 2 minutes.

Each serving provides:

136	Calories	24 g	Carbohydrate
7 g	Protein	237 mg	Sodium
1 g	Fat	2 mg	Cholesterol
2 g	Dietary Fiber		

Ratatouille Soup

Grilling is a wonderful way to cook vegetables. Those of you who think you don't like vegetables should try them grilled or roasted—I was surprised how delicious they can be.

Makes 8 servings

3	small onions, thickly sliced
1	green pepper, cut in half and seeds cleaned out
1	red pepper, cut in half and seeds cleaned out
2	zucchini, cut in half lengthwise
1	eggplant, cut in 1/2-inch rounds
2	teaspoons virgin olive oil
5	cloves garlic, chopped
1/2	teaspoon red pepper flakes
	vegetable spray
2	tablespoons chopped fresh basil (or 2 teaspoons dried)
1	tablespoon fresh oregano (or 1 teaspoon dried)
1/4	cup chopped fresh parsley
1	teaspoon sugar
3	large tomatoes, peeled, seeded, and diced
1/2	pound mushrooms, sliced
21/2	cups chicken stock, defatted (see page 6)
1/2	cup red wine
	salt and pepper to taste
	fresh grated Parmesan cheese for garnish
	fresh chopped parsley for garnish

Put onions, peppers, zucchini, and eggplant in a bowl. Sprinkle with olive oil. Grill the vegetables over hot coals. Really blacken the peppers. Remove peppers and put into a zipped plastic bag and set aside for 10 minutes. Remove the rest of the vegetables and dice. Remove peppers from bag and peel. Remove seeds and stems and dice up peppers.

Sauté the garlic and red pepper flakes in a little vegetable spray. Add grilled vegetables and the rest of ingredients except parsley and Parmesan cheese, and cook on low heat for 30 minutes. Salt and pepper to taste and sprinkle with Parmesan cheese and fresh parsley.

❖

Each serving provides:

83	Calories	13 g	Carbohydrate
4 g	Protein	182 mg	Sodium
2 g	Fat	2 mg	Cholesterol
3 g	Dietary Fiber		

CREAMY MUSHROOM SOUP WITH SPINACH

This is an elegant and soothing soup.

Makes 8 servings

2	heads of garlic, roasted
2	cups nonfat milk
3	cups chicken stock, defatted (see page 6)
4	cups diced, small white mushrooms
1/4	cup chopped celery leaves
2	tablespoons chopped fresh tarragon
2	large potatoes, peeled and shredded
3	green onions, sliced
	butter-flavored vegetable spray
2 1/2	cups chopped fresh spinach
	salt and pepper to taste
2	tablespoons brandy
	croutons and fresh chopped parsley for garnish

Roast garlic by cutting top off 2 heads of garlic. Put garlic heads into an ovenproof dish that just holds the garlic. Add 3 tablespoons chicken broth to the garlic, cover with foil, and cook in a 300° oven for 1 1/2 hours. When garlic is done, squeeze out garlic and mash.

Whisk milk and stock into the mashed garlic and blend well. Add 3 cups of the mushrooms, celery leaves, tarragon, and potatoes and cook 20 minutes. Purée mixture.

Sauté the last cup of mushrooms and green onions in butter-flavored vegetable spray and cook until mushrooms soften.

Add puréed mixture to mushroom-onion mixture. Cook 10
minutes. Add spinach and salt and pepper to taste and cook 5
minutes. Stir in brandy. Ladle into soup bowls and garnish with
croutons and fresh parsley.

Each serving provides:

118	Calories	20 g	Carbohydrate
6 g	Protein	257 mg	Sodium
2 g	Fat	2 mg	Cholesterol
3 g	Dietary Fiber		

FennEl Soup with Baked Onions

There are lots of onions in this recipe but they are mild and delicious because they are baked. Try baking onions like this and adding them to your mashed potatoes—yum!

Makes 8 servings

2	onions, skin left on and left whole
1/2	teaspoon cracked pepper
1/2	cup plus 4 cups chicken stock, defatted (see page 6)
1	cup nonfat milk
4	fennel bulbs, sliced
3	large potatoes, peeled and diced
1	carrot, shredded
1	cup lite evaporated milk
	salt and pepper to taste
	feathery fennel on top of bulbs for garnish

Preheat oven to 325°.

Put onions in a pan and sprinkle with pepper. Add 1/2 cup chicken stock and cover pan with foil. Bake in oven for 1 1/2 hours. Remove onion and squeeze out. Purée onion.

Whisk onion purée into milk and 4 cups of stock. Add fennel, potatoes, and carrot and cook 30 minutes. Stir in evaporated milk and season with salt and pepper. Garnish each dish with fresh fennel.

Each serving provides:

110	Calories	22 g	Carbohydrate
6 g	Protein	229 mg	Sodium
0 g	Fat	4 mg	Cholesterol
2 g	Dietary Fiber		

Grilled Corn Soup

By grilling the corn over smokey coals, this soup develops a beautiful rich flavor. I like to use hickory chips spread over my coals for extra flavor.

Makes 10 servings

8	cobs of corn, husks removed
	butter-flavored vegetable spray
1	onion, chopped
3	cloves garlic, chopped
1	green pepper, minced
1/2	teaspoon red pepper flakes
1	carrot, grated
2	tomatoes, peeled, seeded, and diced
5	cups chicken stock, defatted (see page 6)
1/4	cup flour whisked with 2 cups nonfat milk
	hot sauce to taste
2	tablespoons chopped fresh cilantro
1/2	cup lite evaporated milk
	salt and pepper to taste

Spray corn with the butter-flavored spray. Grill corn over hot coals, turning until a nice color lines the corn. (It takes only a few minutes to grill corn without the husks.) Remove the kernels with a knife and scrape milky residue from cobs into a soup pot. Add corn kernels.

In a nonstick pan that is very hot, add onion, garlic, pepper, and red pepper flakes and dry-fry until browned. Stir constantly so it does not burn. When vegetables have begun to brown, add to soup pot.

Add carrot, tomatoes, stock, flour and milk mixture, and hot sauce. Cook 1 hour. Add cilantro and evaporated milk and season with salt and pepper. Cook over very low heat, gently, until well blended.

❖

Each serving provides:

133	Calories	27 g	Carbohydrate
6 g	Protein	199 mg	Sodium
1 g	Fat	3 mg	Cholesterol
3 g	Dietary Fiber		

Butternut and Pineapple Soup with Caraway

Baking vegetables gives them a fantastic burst of flavor. Bake the butternut squash until a fork pierces it easily.

Makes 10 servings

2	small butternut squash
2	tablespoons sugar
1	medium onion, chopped
1½	cups boiling water
6	cups chicken stock, defatted (see page 6)
1	16-ounce can crushed pineapple, with juice
½	teaspoon powdered ginger
1	teaspoon caraway seed
	dash of nutmeg
	juice of 1 lemon
	salt and pepper to taste
¾	cup lite evaporated milk

Cut squash in half and bake in a 375° oven until done. Scoop out inside of squash and mash. Set aside.

Put sugar and onion in a nonstick stock pot and cook, stirring, until sugar turns a caramel color. Carefully whisk in boiling water and stir until sugar dissolves. Add stock, crushed pineapple with juice, ginger, caraway seed, nutmeg, and lemon juice. Cook mixture 20 minutes, then purée. Return to pan and season with salt and pepper to taste. Carefully stir in evaporated milk and heat over low heat until all is combined.

❖

Each serving provides:

103	Calories	23 g	Carbohydrate
3 g	Protein	171 mg	Sodium
1 g	Fat	3 mg	Cholesterol
3 g	Dietary Fiber		

9

Cold or Fruity Soups

There is nothing so refreshing on a hot summer day than a wonderful cold soup. Many chilled soups take on a beautiful color, so they are as delightful to look at as they are to devour.

With the bountiful selection of summer fruits and vegetables, the possibilities for luscious soups are infinite. I love summer walks with my children when we pick buckets full of wild berries. Or the trips to local farms that let us pick our own peaches, cherries, nectarines, plums, or apricots. Fruit and vegetable stands also offer endless selections. And, of course, living in the part of California that I do enables me to enjoy beautiful fruit trees and lush vegetable gardens in my own yard.

Even if you are not accustomed to cold or fruity soups, I hope you will give a few of these recipes a try. I am sure you will become a devoted fan.

Cranberry Grand Marnier Soup

It is a good idea to freeze some fresh cranberries when they are in season so you can enjoy this soup—and any other favorite cranberry recipes—all year long.

Makes 4 servings

3	cups fresh cranberries
1	cup orange juice
2	teaspoons orange rind
1	cup sugar (or to taste)
3	whole mint leaves (plus a few for garnish)
1	cinnamon stick
1/3	cup Grand Marnier
1/2	cup nonfat sour cream

Put cranberries, orange juice, rind, sugar, mint leaves, and cinnamon stick into a pan and bring to a boil, stirring until all sugar is dissolved. Cook 10 minutes, or until cranberries pop. Remove cinnamon stick and mint leaves. Purée mixture. Stir in Grand Marnier and chill.

When ready to serve, stir in sour cream and garnish with a fresh mint leaf.

❖

Each serving provides:

312	Calories	71 g	Carbohydrate
3 g	Protein	23 mg	Sodium
0 g	Fat	0 mg	Cholesterol
4 g	Dietary Fiber		

Apricot and Pineapple Refresher

When your apricot trees overproduce, you'll appreciate this beautiful summer soup.

Makes 6 servings

2¹/₂	pounds apricots, washed, halved, and pits removed
	juice of 2 lemons
¹/₂	cup apricot nectar
1	8-ounce can crushed pineapple, drained and juice reserved
¹/₂	cup sugar
2	tablespoons minced fresh mint
2	tablespoons arrowroot mixed with reserved pineapple juice
¹/₈	teaspoon nutmeg
¹/₃	cup nonfat sour cream
¹/₂	cup *each* lite evaporated milk and champagne
	fresh mint leaves for garnish

Cook apricots, lemon juice, nectar, pineapple, sugar, and mint until apricots are soft. Purée and stir in arrowroot mixture. Cook over low heat until mixture thickens, then let cool.

In a bowl, mix the nutmeg, sour cream, and evaporated milk. Blend into cool soup and chill. Just before serving, stir in champagne and garnish with a mint leaf.

Each serving provides:

232	Calories	52 g	Carbohydrate
5 g	Protein	37 mg	Sodium
1 g	Fat	1 mg	Cholesterol
5 g	Dietary Fiber		

Blackberry and Lemon Cream Soup

I am very lucky; I have access to beautiful, large blackberries every summer. I love them.

Makes 6 servings

8	cups fresh blackberries
$1/3$	to $1/2$ cup sugar (depending on sweetness of berries)
$1^1/2$	tablespoons cornstarch
2	tablespoons lemon juice
1	cup lemon nonfat yogurt
	rind of 1 lemon
$1/4$	cup nonfat sour cream
1	cup non-dairy topping (such as Cool Whip®)
3	tablespoons blackberry-flavored brandy
	a few fresh blackberries for garnish

Wash berries and put in a pan with sugar, cornstarch, and lemon juice. Cook, stirring constantly, until mixture thickens. Strain through a fine sieve or cheesecloth to remove seeds. Let mixture cool, then chill 4 hours. Stir in yogurt, lemon rind, sour cream, and non-dairy topping, blending well. Stir in brandy and serve with a few fresh, whole berries in each bowl.

❖

Each serving provides:

252	Calories	51 g	Carbohydrate
4 g	Protein	33 mg	Sodium
4 g	Fat	1 mg	Cholesterol
8 g	Dietary Fiber		

BlAck CHERRy Soup
wiTH KiRscH

We have cherry trees in our back yard and how we love harvesting their beautiful, full flavored fruit. If you cannot obtain really dark, sweet cherries it may be preferable to use frozen.

Makes 6 servings

2	pounds dark cherries, pitted
2	cups lemonade (minus 1/4 cup to blend with cornstarch)
	sugar as needed (depending on sweetness of cherries)
3	tablespoons cornstarch (blended with 1/4 cup lemonade)
1	tablespoon grenadine
1/2	cup rosé wine
1/3	cup kirsch
1	cup lite evaporated milk
1/3	cup nonfat sour cream
	fresh mint leaves for garnish

Put cherries and lemonade into a pan and cook 5 minutes, or until cherries soften. Taste and add sugar if too tart. (Do not add too much because we will be adding grenadine.) Purée mixture and return to pan. Be sure that the cherries are very hot and then turn off heat. Blend cornstarch with lemonade until cornstarch is dissolved. Stir into cherry mixture and return heat to low. Cook a few minutes until cherries thicken, and remove from heat. Put into a bowl, cover, let cool. Stir in other ingredi-

❖

ents and blend well. Chill until very cold. Stir thoroughly before serving. Ladle into bowls and garnish with a couple of fresh mint leaves.

❖

Each serving provides:

375	Calories	73 g	Carbohydrate
9 g	Protein	96 mg	Sodium
2 g	Fat	3 mg	Cholesterol
5 g	Dietary Fiber		

PEACH SOUP WITH AMARETTO CREAM

Is there anything better than a perfectly ripe peach? This soup lets the juicy, sweet flavor of the peach shine through.

Makes 6 servings

6	cups peeled and sliced peaches
	juice of 2 lemons
1/3	cup sugar (more if peaches are not sweet enough)
2	cinnamon sticks
2	tablespoons arrowroot mixed with 1/2 cup sparkling water
3/4	cup lite evaporated milk
1/4	cup plus 2 tablespoons Amaretto
1/2	cup non-dairy topping (such as Cool Whip®)
2	tablespoons nonfat sour cream
1/2	teaspoon cinnamon

Purée peaches. Put into a pan and add lemon juice, sugar, cinnamon sticks, and arrowroot mixture. Cook, stirring constantly, until sugar dissolves and mixture thickens. Stir in 1/4 cup Amaretto and the evaporated milk. Let cool, then remove cinnamon stick. Chill mixture.

Mix non-dairy topping, sour cream, cinnamon, and 2 table-spoons Amaretto. Serve soup with a heaping spoonful of the Amaretto cream mixture.

❖

Each serving provides:

214	Calories	43 g	Carbohydrate
5 g	Protein	54 mg	Sodium
2 g	Fat	2 mg	Cholesterol
3 g	Dietary Fiber		

Cold Nectarine Soup with Plum Wine

The nectarine is one of my favorite fruits. I love them in tarts, cobblers, or salads—and they are very refreshing in this chilled soup.

Makes 6 servings

5	nectarines, peeled, pitted, and cut into large pieces
3/4	cup plum wine
1/4	cup lemon juice
3	tablespoons sugar (or to taste)
1/2	cup lite non-dairy topping (such as Cool Whip®), mixed with 1/2 cup low-fat vanilla yogurt
1	nectarine, very thinly sliced, for garnish

Put 5 nectarines into a food processor and purée until smooth. Transfer to a pan and stir in wine, lemon juice, and sugar. Cook, stirring, until sugar dissolves and flavors are well blended. Remove soup to a bowl and let cool. Chill 1 hour.

Mix non-dairy topping and vanilla yogurt until well blended and stir into nectarine mixture. Chill several hours. When ready to serve, do not peel but slice 1 last nectarine very thinly. Spread a few slices on top of each bowl of soup.

❖

Each serving provides:

145	Calories	28 g	Carbohydrate
2 g	Protein	13 mg	Sodium
2 g	Fat	1 mg	Cholesterol
2 g	Dietary Fiber		

Minty Watermelon Delight

You need a really ripe, sweet watermelon for this delightful soup.

Makes 8 servings

1/4	cup mint leaves
3	teaspoons arrowroot
1	cup good white zinfandel
6	cups puréed watermelon
2	tablespoons grenadine
	juice of 1 lemon
1/2	cup light rum (optional)
	sugar to taste
2	cups very tiny watermelon balls
	nonfat sour cream

Put mint leaves, arrowroot, and zinfandel in a pan and blend well. Bring to a boil, stir, and as soon as it thickens remove from heat and let sit 5 minutes. Strain and discard mint leaves. Let mixture come to room temperature.

Put watermelon, grenadine, lemon juice, optional rum, and zinfandel mixture into a bowl, blend well, and chill. Taste and correct seasoning with sugar. Stir in watermelon balls and serve with a dab of sour cream and a mint leaf.

❖

Each serving provides:

132	Calories	23 g	Carbohydrate
2 g	Protein	10 mg	Sodium
1 g	Fat	0 mg	Cholesterol
1 g	Dietary Fiber		

Raspberry Smoothie

Berries are the reason I look forward to the summer months—there is nothing as wonderful as fresh-picked berries. If you live anywhere near a berry thicket, make sure to take your bucket and pick as many as you can. If you are like me and my son, T.J., you will have stained hands and clothes by the time you are finished, as though you ate many more berries than you picked.

Makes 8 servings

6	cups fresh raspberries, puréed
1/3	cup sugar
2	tablespoons cornstarch
1	cup fresh raspberries, slightly crushed
1/2	cup rosé wine
3	tablespoons Chambord liqueur
2	tablespoons grenadine
1/2	cup lite non-dairy topping (such as Cool Whip®)
1/2	cup nonfat vanilla yogurt
	a few whole raspberries and fresh mint leaves for garnish

Put puréed raspberries, sugar, and cornstarch into a pan and heat, stirring, until mixture thickens. Let cool. Add crushed raspberries, wine, Chambord, and grenadine. Chill. When

ready to serve, mix non-dairy topping and vanilla yogurt together and fold into raspberry mixture. Garnish with a whole
raspberry and a mint leaf.

❖

Each serving provides:

132	Calories	28 g	Carbohydrate
2 g	Protein	15 mg	Sodium
2 g	Fat	0 mg	Cholesterol
3 g	Dietary Fiber		

Cool aNd Fruity
StrawbERRY-BaNaNa Soup

This is a gorgeous soup for a spring luncheon.

Makes 6 servings

4	cups puréed strawberries
2	small bananas
2	tablespoons lemon juice
1/2	cup strawberry-banana nectar
1/2	cup blush wine
3	tablespoons honey
1/2	cup nonfat sour cream

Purée the strawberries, bananas, lemon juice, and nectar together. Put into a bowl with wine and honey. Stir to blend. Carefully whisk in sour cream and chill. Whisk again before serving.

Each serving provides:

147	Calories	32 g	Carbohydrate
3 g	Protein	17 mg	Sodium
1 g	Fat	0 mg	Cholesterol
5 g	Dietary Fiber		

CREAMY BEET SOUP

The pink color of this soup is as lovely to look at as it is delicious to eat.

Makes 8 servings

1/2	cup chopped onion
1	cup sliced leeks, white part only
1	teaspoon sugar
2	teaspoons unsalted butter
2	tablespoons flour
2	cups hot water
2	cups apple juice
2	cups *each* diced beets and apples
1/2	cup sherry
1/2	cup lite evaporated milk
1/3	cup nonfat sour cream
	salt and pepper to taste

Sauté onion, leeks, and sugar in butter until onion and sugar begin to caramelize. Blend in flour and whisk in water and apple juice. When blended well, add beets, apples, and sherry. Bring to a boil, then simmer 40 minutes. Purée mixture. Put mixture into a bowl and stir in evaporated milk and sour cream. Season with salt and pepper. Chill.

❖

Each serving provides:

138	Calories	23 g	Carbohydrate
3 g	Protein	187 mg	Sodium
3 g	Fat	7 mg	Cholesterol
2 g	Dietary Fiber		

Cold Cucumber Fennel Soup

I love this soup. Sometimes I add 1 cup of little cooked shrimp to it to make it look really pretty.

Makes 6 servings

3	cucumbers, peeled, seeded, and chopped large (reserve 1/4 cup and dice small)
2	fennel bulbs, 1 chopped large
3	center celery stalks chopped, with leaves attached
3	cups chicken stock, defatted (see page 6)
1	tablespoon fresh fennel greens
2	tablespoons flour mixed with 1/2 cup very hot water
1	green onion, minced
1/2	cup lite evaporated milk mixed with 1/2 cup nonfat plain yogurt
	salt and fresh ground pepper to taste
	fennel sprigs for garnish

Put cucumbers, chopped fennel bulbs, celery, and stock in a pan and cook 15 to 20 minutes, or until vegetables are soft. Purée in blender or processor. Add fennel greens, flour and water mixture, and green onion. Cook until mixture thickens. Refrigerate until thoroughly chilled.

❖

Before serving, combine evaporated milk and yogurt and mix into chilled soup. Season with salt and pepper to taste. Serve garnished with a few sprigs of fennel.

❖

Each serving provides:

74	Calories	14 g	Carbohydrate
4 g	Protein	215 mg	Sodium
1 g	Fat	3 mg	Cholesterol
3 g	Dietary Fiber		

10

Vegetable Stews

A s a child, I remember coming home after school and smelling the savory scents of my mother's lamb stew, her pot roast, or her wonderful drunken chicken stew. Today my children enjoy those same comforting aromas that link us to thoughts of family gathering around the table, enjoying each other's company over a heartwarming meal. I think it is so important to pass our heritage from generation to generation, and how better to do this than through food? Even with our ever-changing American tastes, there are certain foods that will survive all metamorphosis.

Stews are really great for today's working families who want to come home and have a wonderful, easy, substantial meal. Most of these recipes take only a few simple steps before they can be put into a Crock-pot or thrown into the oven, while you go about your busy day.

My passion for vegetables extends to developing many luscious, hearty stews using numerous intriguing combinations of vegetables. Vegetables simmered slowly in a flavorful liquid develop a rich, delightful taste. Many people prefer to use frozen or canned vegetables in their stews because of the convenience.

--- ❖ ---

Granted, it is easier and quicker, but fresh vegetables are almost as easy to prepare and they are so much more healthful, splendid, and colorful. It takes just a little bit of time to clean and prepare fresh vegetables, and if you have a mandolin slicer or a food processor, the job is even faster. For most stews, however, I prefer large chunks of vegetables—to define color and taste. For this I just turn to my trusty knife.

SWEET POTATO STEW

This stew has a rich, delicious taste due to the sweetness of the fruit stock.

Makes 8 servings

2	pounds sweet potatoes, peeled and cut into 1-inch dice
1	onion, cut into thin wedges and separated
3	cloves garlic, chopped
3	teaspoons unsalted butter
3	stalks celery, cut in 1 1/2-inch slices
2	carrots, cut in 1/2-inch slices
1	cup tomatoes, diced small
1/4	cup chopped fresh parsley
1	teaspoon dried thyme
1 1/2	cups vegetable stock (see page 12)
1 1/2	cups fruit stock (see page 15)
1	yellow pepper, cut into 1-inch dice
1	cup peas
2	tablespoons cornstarch mixed with 1/4 cup lemon juice
	salt and fresh ground pepper to taste

Put diced sweet potatoes in water until ready to use.

Sauté onion and garlic in butter until onion is transparent. Add sweet potatoes, celery, carrots, tomatoes, parsley, thyme, and stocks. Cook 30 minutes. Add pepper and peas and cook 10 minutes more. Stir in cornstarch mixture and cook until liquid begins to thicken. Season with salt and pepper to taste.

❖

Each serving provides:

185	Calories	39 g	Carbohydrate
4 g	Protein	191 mg	Sodium
2 g	Fat	4 mg	Cholesterol
5 g	Dietary fiber		

GINGERY WINTER SQUASH STEW

The colors of this stew make a colorful fall sight.

Makes 8 servings

1	large onion, cut into thin wedges and separated
2	leeks, white part only, sliced
2	cloves garlic
1	tablespoon brown sugar
2	teaspoons unsalted butter
1	tablespoon minced fresh ginger
1	cup stock, defatted (see page 6)
2	tablespoons flour
1	large green pepper, cut in 1-inch dice
1	large yellow pepper, cut in 1-inch dice
3	cups 2-inch diced butternut squash
3	cups 2-inch diced acorn squash
1/2	cup Madeira
1/2	cup fruit stock (see page 15) or orange juice
1 1/2	cups chicken stock, defatted (see page 6)
1/4	cup chopped fresh parsley
2	tablespoons lemon juice
	salt and fresh ground pepper

Preheat oven to 375°.

Put onion, leeks, garlic, sugar, butter, ginger, 1 cup chicken stock, and flour into a nonstick pan and cook over low heat until mixture thickens. Put onion mixture and rest of ingredi-

ents (except salt and pepper) into a roasting pan, cover, and
cook until vegetables begin to be done. Remove cover and cook
30 minutes more. Season to taste with salt and pepper.

❖

Each serving provides:

92	Calories	17 g	Carbohydrate
3 g	Protein	146 mg	Sodium
1 g	Fat	4 mg	Cholesterol
3 g	Dietary fiber		

Sweet Potato, Pear, and Apple Stew

A crisp, green salad and delicious bread along with this stew makes a great vegetarian meal.

Makes 8 servings

2	medium onions, chopped
2	tablespoons sugar
2	tablespoons flour
2	teaspoons unsalted butter
1 1/2	cups vegetable stock (see page 12)
1/2	cup white wine
1 1/2	pounds sweet potatoes, peeled and cut into 1-inch slices
1	large fennel bulb, cut into thin wedges
1	20-ounce can pineapple chunks with juice
1	tablespoon fresh thyme
1	teaspoon fresh ground pepper
1 1/2	pounds apples, peeled, cored, and cut into 8 wedges
1 1/2	pounds pears, peeled, cored, and cut into 1/2-inch dice
	salt to taste
1	tablespoon dark rum

Sauté onions with sugar, flour, and butter in a nonstick pan for 2 minutes. Whisk in vegetable stock and wine. Add sweet potatoes, fennel, pineapple with juice, thyme, and pepper. Cover and simmer until potatoes are tender. Add apples and pears and cook 10 minutes more, or until fruit is tender. Season with salt and stir in rum.

Each serving provides:

246	Calories	57 g	Carbohydrate
3 g	Protein	151 mg	Sodium
2 g	Fat	3 mg	Cholesterol
6 g	Dietary fiber		

Pumpkin Vegetable Stew

I look forward with great anticipation to seasonal food. However, today so many foods are becoming available all year round. It takes a lot of the fun out of waiting. At least I can still look forward to fall to cook with fresh pumpkin.

Makes 8 servings

2	teaspoons butter
1	onion, cut in thin wedges and separated
2	leeks, white part only, sliced
2	carrots, sliced
2	tablespoons brown sugar
2	cups peeled and cut into 1-inch dice pumpkin
1	yellow pepper, diced large
1	green pepper, diced large
2	cups cooked white beans, drained (mash 1 cup to thicken stew)
2	small parsnips, peeled and sliced
1¹/₂	teaspoons thyme
1	tablespoon curry powder
2	tablespoons chopped fresh parsley
1	cup vegetable stock (see page 12)
1	cup fruit stock (see page 15)
¹/₂	cup Marsala
	salt and pepper to taste
	chopped fresh parsley for garnish

Preheat oven to 375°.

Melt butter in a nonstick pan and sauté onion, leeks, and carrots for 5 minutes. Sprinkle with brown sugar and cook 2 more minutes. Add pumpkin, peppers, beans, mashed beans, parsnips, thyme, curry powder, parsley, stocks, and Marsala. Cook in oven 30 minutes, or until vegetables are done. Serve with a sprinkling of parsley.

❖

Each serving provides:

167	Calories	30 g	Carbohydrate
6 g	Protein	294 mg	Sodium
2 g	Fat	3 mg	Cholesterol
5 g	Dietary Fiber		

CRUNCHY BROCCOLI AND CAULIFLOWER STEW

This is a delicious, change of pace dish with an Oriental flair.

Makes 8 servings

1	cup onion, cut in wedges and separated
2	cloves garlic, chopped
2	teaspoons chopped fresh ginger
1/4	teaspoon red pepper flakes
2	teaspoons sesame oil
1	pound broccoli, cut into flowerets, stems peeled and sliced
2	cups cauliflower flowerets
1	cup peeled and diced Jerusalem artichokes (dropped into water with added lemon juice as soon as they are cut)
1	large red pepper, diced large
1	8-ounce can sliced water chestnuts
1/4	cup chopped Chinese basil (or regular basil)
1	tablespoon lite soy sauce
1	teaspoon white pepper
2	cups chicken stock, defatted (see page 6)
1/2	cup white wine
	salt to taste
1	tablespoon arrowroot mixed with 3 tablespoons water

Sauté onion, garlic, ginger, and red pepper flakes in sesame oil until onion is soft. Add all other ingredients, except salt and arrowroot mixture, and simmer on stove 20 minutes. Season to taste with salt and pepper then thicken with arrowroot mixture.

Each serving provides:

227	Calories	48 g	Carbohydrate
7 g	Protein	165 mg	Sodium
2 g	Fat	1 mg	Cholesterol
4 g	Dietary fiber		

Smokey Turnip Stew

This stew can be thickened with cornstarch or arrowroot mixed with a little water, if you desire a thicker stew.

Makes 6 servings

1	tablespoon butter
3	leeks, white part only, sliced
3	tablespoons flour
3	medium potatoes, peeled and cut in 1/2-inch dice
3	cups vegetable stock (see page 12)
1/2	cup dry vermouth
2	carrots, diced
2	cups peeled and diced tomato
1	pound turnips, cut in 1/2-inch dice
1	10-ounce package frozen lima beans, thawed
1	bay leaf
1/4	teaspoon liquid smoke flavoring
1/4	cup chopped fresh parsley
1	teaspoon dried marjoram
1	teaspoon fresh ground pepper
	salt and pepper to taste
	chopped fresh parsley for garnish

In a heavy pan, sauté leeks in butter for 3 minutes. Sprinkle with flour and blend. Add potatoes, stock, vermouth, and carrots to the leeks. Stir until well blended. Cook, covered, 15 min-

utes. Add rest of ingredients, except salt and pepper, and cook
15 minutes more. Remove bay leaf. Season with salt and pepper, garnish with chopped parsley.

Each serving provides:

264	Calories	52 g	Carbohydrate
8 g	Protein	826 mg	Sodium
3 g	Fat	6 mg	Cholesterol
7 g	Dietary fiber		

Your Favorite Greens Stew

Greens include mustard greens, kale, collards, beet greens, turnip greens, dandelion greens, spinach, and swiss chard. Greens are usually mixed in recipes: strong-flavored greens mixed with milder-flavored greens. If you like the bitter greens—such as dandelion greens, turnip greens, or mustard greens—it helps to blanch them before adding to a recipe.

Makes 8 servings

1	large onion, diced
3	cloves garlic, chopped
1	tablespoon butter
1	tablespoon flour
2	cups beef stock, defatted (see page 10)
$1/2$	cup vermouth
2	cups diced potatoes
1	cup diced carrots
1	cup diced celery
$1/4$	teaspoon liquid smoke flavoring
$1/2$	teaspoon dried thyme
3	cups mixed greens, chopped
	fresh ground pepper and salt to taste
	grated Parmesan cheese for garnish

In a large pot, sauté onion and garlic in butter, very slowly, until onion is transparent. Sprinkle with flour and mix. Add stock and vermouth and blend well. Add potatoes, carrots, celery, smoke flavoring, and thyme and cook about 20 minutes.

Add greens and cook 15 minutes more. Season with salt and pepper. Sprinkle each serving with a teaspoon of grated Parmesan cheese.

Each serving provides:

108	Calories	16 g	Carbohydrate
4 g	Protein	224 mg	Sodium
3 g	Fat	7 mg	Cholesterol
2 g	Dietary fiber		

Fresh Peas and Tomato Stew

I have fond memories of sitting with my grandmother shelling peas and listening to her many tales. One pound of whole peas equals about 1 1/4 cup shelled peas.

Makes 8 servings

1/2	cup chopped onion
1	tablespoon butter
1	tablespoon flour
1/2	cup white wine
3	tomatoes, peeled and chopped
1	cup chopped mushrooms
1	pound little red new potatoes, peeled
1	cup artichoke hearts in water, drained
1	tablespoon chopped fresh tarragon
2	cups beef stock, defatted (see page 10)
1/4	teaspoon liquid smoke flavoring
3 1/2	cups fresh peas, shelled
	fresh ground pepper and salt to taste
	chopped fresh parsley for garnish

Sauté onion in butter 1 minute. Add flour and stir until all flour disappears. Whisk in wine then add tomatoes, mushrooms, potatoes, artichokes hearts, tarragon, stock, and smoke flavoring. Cook 40 minutes. Add fresh peas, salt and pepper to taste, and cook 8 more minutes. Garnish with fresh parsley.

Each serving provides:

144	Calories	26 g	Carbohydrate
7 g	Protein	242 mg	Sodium
2 g	Fat	6 mg	Cholesterol
4 g	Dietary fiber		

Crock-pot Adaptation

11

MEATY STEWS

B lustery nights make us want to get cozy and enjoy robust warming meals. These stews make the perfect center-piece for such a meal. Meats become moist and tender with long cooking. Many of these dishes can be made in a Crock-pot so your meal will be waiting for you when you want it.

Everyone seems to eat less meat these days, with good rea-son, since it is high in saturated fats and cholesterol. But there are still those who hunger for it; and we know that if meat is eaten in moderation it can be a satisfying part of our healthful diets. To eat healthy and maintain a good diet, you need not limit the kinds of foods you eat, just the portions.

The USDA understands our concerns about the quality of meat we consume. Nowadays there are delicious lean cuts of meat available to us. When we remove all visible fat and slice meat in small portions we are decreasing the fat content and calories. We decrease the amount of meat in these stews and in-crease the amount of vegetables to make a hearty portion of stew.

Any time you want the wonderful old-time favorite re-cipes, use a variety of meats and enhance them with fragrant herbs, spices, and a cornucopia of beautiful vegetables. Providing choices like this and keeping recipes filling and fascinating is the goal of healthful delicious eating.

Teriyaki Beef Stew

Teriyaki is a wonderful flavor for a stew.

Makes 4 servings

1 1/2	tablespoons lite soy sauce
1 1/2	cups beef stock, defatted (see page 10)
1 1/2	tablespoons sherry
1/4	cup pineapple juice
1	teaspoon grated fresh ginger
1/2	teaspoon garlic powder
1/2	pound sirloin, thinly sliced
	vegetable spray
1	carrot, thinly sliced, diagonally
1/2	cup white rice
3	green onions, cut into 1 1/2-inch lengths, diagonally
1/2	cup snap peas

Put soy sauce, beef stock, sherry, pineapple juice, ginger, and garlic powder into a bowl and mix well.

Sauté sirloin in a nonstick pan sprayed with vegetable spray until meat is only slightly pink. Pour in stock mixture, carrot, and white rice. Cover and cook 20 minutes. Add green onions and snap peas and cook for 5 minutes longer.

Each serving provides:

270	Calories	27 g	Carbohydrate
15 g	Protein	277 mg	Sodium
11 g	Fat	40 mg	Cholesterol
2 g	Dietary Fiber		

Mexican Beef Jalapeño Stew

The leftovers from this stew make great burritos.

Makes 6 servings

1	pound lean beef, thinly sliced
2	cups peeled and diced tomato
1	large onion, diced
4	cloves garlic, minced
1	or 2 jalapeño peppers, diced small
1/4	cup chopped fresh cilantro
1	teaspoon dried oregano
1	bay leaf
2	cups water
1/2	teaspoon cumin
2	large potatoes, diced
1	cup corn kernels
	salt to taste

Put beef, tomato, onion, garlic, jalapeños, cilantro, oregano, bay leaf, water, and cumin into a covered casserole. Cook 30 minutes. Add potatoes and cook 20 minutes more. Add corn and cook 10 to 15 minutes more. Season with salt to taste. Remove bay leaf and discard.

❖

Each serving provides:

281	Calories	22 g	Carbohydrate
18 g	Protein	192 mg	Sodium
14 g	Fat	51 mg	Cholesterol
3 g	Dietary Fiber		

Oriental Beef and Black Bean Stew

I love this stew—but watch the sodium.

Makes 6 servings

1	pound lean sirloin, cut into small dice
1	teaspoon sesame oil
2¹/₂	cups cooked black beans
1	cup peeled and diced potatoes
¹/₂	cup diced green onion
3	cloves garlic, minced
1	hot red pepper, minced
1	teaspoon sugar
¹/₂	teaspoon grated fresh ginger
¹/₂	cup catsup
1	cup tomato sauce
1	cup beef stock, defatted (see page 10)
1	tablespoon lite soy sauce
1	tablespoon oyster sauce

In an ovenproof pan with a lid, sauté sirloin in sesame oil until it just begins to turn color. Add rest of ingredients and mix well. Cover pan and bake 50 to 60 minutes.

Each serving provides:

356	Calories	33 g	Carbohydrate
23 g	Protein	714 mg	Sodium
15 g	Fat	52 mg	Cholesterol
5 g	Dietary Fiber		

Crock-pot Adaptation

Follow recipe, but put into Crock-pot after browning meat. Cook on high 4 to 4½ hours.

Pork-U-Pine Stew

This may look like a lot of ingredients, but they are for both meatballs and a sauce. This is a very delightful stew.

Makes 6 servings

1/2	pound lean ground pork
1/2	cup cooked rice
1/4	cup minced onion
1	clove garlic, minced
2	tablespoons chopped fresh parsley
1	teaspoon crushed dried rosemary
1/2	teaspoon salt
1	teaspoon pepper
1/4	cup egg substitute
	vegetable spray
2 1/2	cups tomato sauce
1/2	cup red wine
1/2	cup water
2	teaspoons Italian seasoning
1	tablespoon Worcestershire sauce
1	teaspoon beef soup base (or 1 bouillon cube)
1/4	pound green beans, cut into 1-inch lengths
2	carrots, cut into chunks
2	parsnips, cut into chunks
1	green bell pepper, cut into chunks
	salt and pepper to taste

Preheat oven to 375°.

Mix ground pork, rice, onion, garlic, parsley, rosemary, salt, pepper, and egg substitute together. When mixed well, make 1-inch balls until all the mixture is used. Put the meatballs on a cookie sheet sprayed with vegetable spray and bake until lightly browned. Remove to a Dutch oven with a lid.

Put the tomato sauce, wine, water, Italian seasoning, Worcestershire sauce, and soup base into the casserole and mix well. Add meatballs, green beans, carrots, parsnips, and peppers. Cover. Bake 40 minutes. Season with salt and pepper.

Each serving provides:

234	Calories	28 g	Carbohydrate
11 g	Protein	1146 mg	Sodium
9 g	Fat	25 mg	Cholesterol
4 g	Dietary Fiber		

HUNGARIAN GOULASH

Paprika comes in sweet and hot flavors. You can add more hot to this recipe if you like it spicy.

Makes 10 servings

2	pounds lean beef, all fat removed and cut into 1-inch squares
1/2	cup flour mixed with 1 teaspoon pepper and 1/2 teaspoon salt
	vegetable spray
1	large onion, cut into wedges and separated
4	cloves garlic, minced
3	tablespoons flour mixed with 2/3 cup very hot water
2	cups beef stock, defatted (see page 10)
1	tablespoon tomato paste
1	cup red wine
2	teaspoons caraway seed
1	tablespoon sweet Hungarian paprika
1/2	teaspoon hot Hungarian paprika (or to taste)
1/4	teaspoon liquid smoke flavoring
1	large red bell pepper, diced
1	pound small red potatoes, halved
	salt and pepper to taste
	chopped fresh flat-leaf parsley for garnish

Preheat oven to 350°.

Dredge beef in flour mixture and brown in a nonstick pan sprayed with vegetable spray. Set aside.

Sauté onion and garlic in more vegetable spray until onion

softens. Stir in flour mixture and cook until smooth. Add stock, tomato paste, wine, caraway seed, paprikas, smoke flavoring, and peppers. Cook for 1 hour in a covered casserole. Remove from oven and add potatoes. Return to oven and cook 30 minutes more. Season with salt and pepper to taste and garnish with parsley.

❖

Each serving provides:

316	Calories	19 g	Carbohydrate
20 g	Protein	307 mg	Sodium
17 g	Fat	62 mg	Cholesterol
2 g	Dietary Fiber		

 Crock-pot Adaptation
Follow instructions until cooking in covered casserole. Instead put ingredients into Crock-pot, adding potatoes at beginning of cooking. Cook on high 4 to 5 hours. Season and garnish.

Curried Lamb Ragout

We don't eat lamb too often because of the fat content. But sometimes you have to splurge to satisfy a yearning.

Makes 10 servings

1 1/2	pounds lamb, all fat removed and cut into 1-inch squares
1/3	cup flour mixed with 1/2 teaspoon salt and pepper
	vegetable spray
1	onion, chopped
3	cloves garlic, minced
2	tablespoons flour mixed with 1/2 cup very hot water
1	to 2 tablespoons curry powder
1 1/2	cups beef stock, defatted (see page 10)
1	cup red wine
1/4	cup mint jelly
1/2	teaspoon ground cardamom
3	small parsnips, peeled and diced
2	yams, peeled and diced
3	zucchini, cut into 1/2-inch slices
1/4	pound green beans, cut into 1-inch lengths
2	carrots, peeled and cut into 1/2-inch slices
	salt and pepper to taste
	chopped fresh parsley for garnish

Preheat oven to 350°.

Dredge meat in flour mixture and sauté in a nonstick pan sprayed with vegetable spray until meat is browned. Set aside.

Sauté onion and garlic in same pan sprayed with vegetable

spray until onion is soft. Add flour and water mixture and stir until blended. Add curry, stock, wine, jelly, and cardamom and cook in oven 1 hour in covered pan. Add rest of ingredients and cook 30 minutes more, or until vegetables are done. Garnish with chopped parsley.

❖

Each serving provides:

239	Calories	30 g	Carbohydrate
17 g	Protein	296 mg	Sodium
6 g	Fat	48 mg	Cholesterol
3 g	Dietary Fiber		

Crock-pot Adaptation
Follow instructions, but put all ingredients (except salt, pepper, and parsley) into Crock-pot and cook on high 5 to 6 hours. Season with salt and pepper and garnish with parsley.

Garbanzo Bean Stew

You can char your peppers on a grill, in the broiler, or on top of a gas stove. Lay pepper on a rack and let char until mostly black and blistery. Drop into a zipped plastic bag, close, and let sit 10 minutes. Remove from bag and peel skin, leaving some of the black on the pepper.

Makes 12 servings

1	pound garbanzo beans, soaked overnight
	water to cover
1 1/2	pounds sirloin, all visible fat removed, and diced
2	charred red peppers, peeled, seeds removed, and diced
1	medium onion, chopped
1	bunch green onions, sliced
1	teaspoon fresh ground pepper
2	cloves garlic, chopped
2	teaspoons virgin olive oil
4	tomatoes, peeled, seeded, and chopped
2	cups tomato sauce
1/2	cup chicken stock, defatted (see page 6)
1/2	cup red wine
1	bay leaf
1	tablespoon paprika
1/2	teaspoon cumin
2	teaspoons thyme
3	cups chopped kale, stems removed
1/2	cup chopped fresh parsley
	salt and pepper to taste
3	tablespoons grated dry jack cheese for garnish
	chopped fresh parsley for garnish

Preheat oven to 325°.

Soak beans overnight in water. In the morning, drain beans, cover with fresh water, and then add 2 more inches of water. Cook beans 2 hours. Drain beans and reserve.

Cook sirloin, peppers, onion, green onions, pepper, and garlic in olive oil until meat is no longer pink. Add tomatoes, tomato sauce, stock, wine, bay leaf, paprika, cumin, thyme, kale, and parsley. Cook in oven 1 1/2 hours. Remove from oven and stir well. Remove bay leaf and discard. Salt and pepper to taste and sprinkle top with grated dry jack cheese and a sprinkling of parsley.

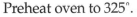

Each serving provides:

322	Calories	31 g	Carbohydrate
20 g	Protein	437 mg	Sodium
14 g	Fat	40 mg	Cholesterol
5 g	Dietary Fiber		

Lamb Shank Stew with Cranberry Beans

This is real old-time comfort food. My father liked to make this dish and refrigerate it overnight to remove any extra fat, then rewarm it the next day. If you do this, you may have to add a little water when rewarming.

Makes 6 servings

6	lamb shanks, all visible fat removed
1/3	cup flour mixed with 1 teaspoon pepper and 1/2 teaspoon salt
	vegetable spray
1	large onion, chopped
2	cloves garlic, minced
1/2	cup chopped carrots
1/2	cup chopped celery
2	teaspoons butter
1	cup cranberry beans, soaked overnight and drained
2	cups tomato sauce
1	cup red wine
1/2	cup water
1	bay leaf
1	teaspoon *each* dried rosemary and thyme
2	tablespoons chopped fresh parsley
	salt and pepper to taste

Preheat oven to 350°.

Dredge shanks in flour mixture and brown in a very hot nonstick pan that has been sprayed with vegetable spray. Set shanks aside.

In same pan, sauté onion, garlic, carrots, and celery in butter until onion is soft. Return shanks to pan with vegetables and add all other ingredients except salt and pepper. Bring mixture to a boil on top of the stove and then cook, covered, in oven for 2 hours. Remove bay leaf. Season with salt and pepper.

Each serving provides:

298	Calories	33 g	Carbohydrate
29 g	Protein	918 mg	Sodium
5 g	Fat	67 mg	Cholesterol
5 g	Dietary Fiber		

Pork and Apricot Stew

Pork is always great when given a fruity taste.

Makes 10 servings

2	1-pound pork tenderloins, all visible fat removed, cut into 1-inch slices
	vegetable spray
1	onion, cut into thin wedges and separated
4	cloves garlic, minced
1	teaspoon rosemary, crushed
1	teaspoon thyme
1	cup dried apricots
2	cups chicken stock (see page 6)
1	cup fruit stock (see page 15)
1	cup port wine
3	small parsnips, peeled and cut into 1/2-inch slices
	salt and pepper to taste
1	tablespoon arrowroot mixed with 2 tablespoons water (optional)

Preheat oven to 350°.

Sauté meat in a nonstick pan sprayed with vegetable spray until meat begins to brown. Remove meat and set aside.

Sauté onion and garlic in same pan sprayed with a little more vegetable spray until onion is transparent.

In a Dutch oven, put pork, onions, garlic, rosemary, thyme, apricots, stocks, port, and parsnips. Cook 1 hour. Season with salt and pepper. Thicken with arrowroot mixture if you want a thicker stew.

❖

Each serving provides:

270	Calories	24 g	Carbohydrate
22 g	Protein	206 mg	Sodium
7 g	Fat	58 mg	Cholesterol
2 g	Dietary Fiber		

Old-Fashioned Beef and Lamb Stew

*When I was young I would really look forward to this delicious stew.
It is a great way to use up leftover coffee. Save your extra coffee and
use it in stews, barbeque sauces and to stew fruit in. It's great!*

Makes 10 servings

1	pound lean beef, fat removed and cut into 1-inch squares
1	pound lean lamb, fat removed and cut into 1-inch squares
1/2	cup flour mixed with 1 teaspoon pepper and 1/2 teaspoon salt
	vegetable spray
1	large onion, cut into thin wedges and separated
2	bay leaves
1	teaspoon dried rosemary
1	teaspoon turmeric
1	cup red wine
1	cup cut up stewed tomatoes
1	cup beef stock, defatted (see page 10)
1	cup strong coffee
1	tablespoon Worcestershire sauce
1	tablespoon flour
1/3	cup chopped fresh parsley
2	turnips, peeled and cut into chunks
2	parsnips, peeled and cut into 1/2-inch slices

1	cup diced carrot
1	cup diced celery
3	pattypan squash, cut into sixths
	salt and pepper to taste

Preheat oven to 375°.

Dredge beef and lamb in flour mixture and sauté meat in a very hot pan sprayed with vegetable spray until meat is browned. To same pan, add onion, bay leaves, rosemary, turmeric, red wine, tomatoes, stock, coffee, Worcestershire sauce, flour, and parsley. Blend well and cook 1 1/2 hours in oven. Remove from oven, add turnips, parsnips, carrot, celery, and squash. Return to oven and cook 30 more minutes, or until vegetables are done. Remove bay leaves. Season with salt and pepper to taste.

Each serving provides:

274	Calories	20 g	Carbohydrate
21 g	Protein	390 mg	Sodium
12 g	Fat	63 mg	Cholesterol
3 g	Dietary Fiber		

Crock-pot Adaptation

Follow instructions through browning meat. Then add all ingredients to Crock-pot and cook on high 5 hours. Remove bay leaves and season to taste.

Beef and Barley Stew with Ale

There is nothing as satisfying as an old-fashioned meal—and this is a family favorite.

Makes 10 servings

2	pounds lean beef, all fat removed and cut into 1-inch dice
1/2	cup flour mixed with 1 1/2 teaspoons pepper and 1/2 teaspoon salt
	vegetable spray
2	cups chopped onion
3	cloves garlic, minced
1	carrot, minced
1	stalk celery, minced
3/4	cup pearl barley
3	stalks celery, cut in 1 1/2-inch lengths
2	carrots, cut in half lengthwise, and cut into 1 1/2-inch lengths
3	potatoes, peeled and cut into chunks
1/3	cup chopped fresh parsley
2	bay leaves
1 1/2	teaspoon thyme
1	teaspoon Italian spices
1	cup tomato sauce
2	cups beef stock, defatted (see page 10)
1 1/2	cups flat ale
1 1/2	teaspoons fresh ground pepper

1/2   pound fresh green beans, cut into 1-inch lengths
2   cobs of fresh corn, cut into 1 1/2-inch lengths
       salt to taste
3   teaspoons arrowroot mixed with 2 tablespoons water
       (optional)
       chopped fresh parsley for garnish

Preheat oven to 350°.

Dredge beef in flour mixture. Sauté in a very hot pan sprayed with vegetable spray until meat is browned. Remove meat and set aside.

In same pan, sauté onion, garlic, carrot, and celery in vegetable spray until onion is soft. Add meat, barley, celery, carrots, potatoes, parsley, bay leaves, thyme, Italian spices, tomato sauce, stock, ale, and pepper. Cook 1 1/2 hours. Add beans, corn, and salt, and continue to cook for 30 to 40 minutes, or until vegetables are done. Remove bay leaves. Thicken with arrowroot mixture if desired. Garnish with fresh parsley.

❖

Each serving provides:

400	Calories	38 g	Carbohydrate
23 g	Protein	473 mg	Sodium
18 g	Fat	62 mg	Cholesterol
6 g	Dietary Fiber		

Crock-pot Adaptation

Follow the instructions until ingredients go into oven. Instead put all ingredients into Crock-pot and add only enough beef stock to cover the ingredients. Cook on high for 4 to 6 hours. Season with salt and pepper and with parsley before serving. Add more stock at the end if necessary.

Corned Beef and Cabbage Stew

*Corned beef is high in sodium, but I couldn't leave out such a classic.
Using eye of the round will cut the fat in this recipe.*

Makes 10 servings

1 1/2	pounds lean corned beef, diced, with eye of the round
	water to cover
2	large onions, slivered
3	cloves garlic, chopped
3	tablespoons vegetable stock
3	tablespoons flour mixed with 1/2 cup very hot water
3	large potatoes, diced large
3	carrots, cut into chunks
3	stalks celery, cut into chunks
1	red pepper, minced
1/3	cup chopped fresh parsley
1/4	teaspoon liquid smoke flavoring
3	tomatoes, peeled and puréed
2	cups vegetable stock (see page 12)
1	12-ounce can flat beer
1	teaspoon pepper
1	small cabbage, cut into small wedges
1	cup diced parsnips
	salt and pepper to taste

Cook beef in water for 1 1/2 hours. Remove meat from water
and set aside.

Sauté onion and garlic in vegetable stock until stock evapo-

rates completely. Sprinkle with flour and water mixture and
cook until smooth. Add meat, potatoes, carrots, celery, peppers,
parsley, smoke flavoring, tomatoes, vegetable stock, beer, and
pepper. Cook 2 hours. Add cabbage and cook 15 minutes. Add
parsnips, season with salt and pepper, and cook for 10 more
minutes. Add more vegetable stock if necessary.

❖

Each serving provides:

233	Calories	26 g	Carbohydrate
12 g	Protein	715 mg	Sodium
10 g	Fat	46 mg	Cholesterol
5 g	Dietary Fiber		

Homemade Sausage Stew

This sausage made into patties is wonderful for breakfast, and delicious used as a stuffing.

Makes 8 servings

1	pound pork tenderloin
3	green onions, minced
4	cloves garlic, minced
1	teaspoon fennel seed
2	teaspoons Italian seasoning
1/4	cup minced green pepper
2	egg whites
1	egg shell full of ice water
2	teaspoons cracked pepper
1/2	teaspoon salt
	vegetable spray
1	cup minced onion
3	tablespoons flour mixed with 1/2 cup hot water
2	cups cooked pinto beans
4	large potatoes, peeled and diced
4	tomatoes, peeled, seeded, and chopped
2	cups 1-inch sliced green beans
1	cup tomato sauce
1	cup beef stock, defatted (see page 10)
1	cup red wine
1	cup large diced cabbage
4	zucchini, diced large
	salt and pepper to taste

Preheat oven to 350°.

Freeze tenderloin for about 2 hours. Remove from freezer and cut into chunks. In your processor, grind pork with the metal blade. If you do not have a food processor, use any kind of grinder.

Put pork into a bowl and add green onions, garlic, fennel seed, Italian seasoning, and peppers and mix well. Add egg whites, ice water, pepper, and salt. Blend well to make sausage. In a nonstick pan sprayed with vegetable spray, fry sausage and break up into chuncks as you cook it. Cook until almost all the pink is gone. Set aside.

In a Dutch oven sprayed with vegetable spray, sauté minced onion until onion is soft. Add flour mixture and blend well. Add sausage, beans, potatoes, tomatoes, green beans, tomato sauce, beef stock, and red wine. Cook in oven 40 minutes. Add cabbage and zucchini and cook about 20 more minutes. Season with salt and pepper.

❖

Each serving provides:

351	Calories	50 g	Carbohydrate
29 g	Protein	523 mg	Sodium
4 g	Fat	54 mg	Cholesterol
8 g	Dietary Fiber		

12

Chicken Stews

C hicken is so versatile and so universally liked, that it is an excellent choice to use in stews. Whether embellishing it with wine, whiskey, tequila, fresh vegetables, fresh or dried fruits, or spices and herbs, chicken always fuses beautifully for a delicious, flavorful dish.

Because we are concentrating on low fat in this book, I use skinless turkey or chicken breasts for these recipes. Keep in mind that white meat cooks very fast. So while our other meat stews can cook for hours, chicken stews never need to cook more than an hour—and some stews need less than that. Since the cooking time is relatively short, I don't recommend all day in a Crock-pot or you will have very tough meat. If you like Crock-pot cooking, a few hours on a very low temperature will be all that you need.

Barbecue Chicken and Pineapple Stew

This is so delicious that it is hard to believe that there is so little fat. It is also incredibly fast and easy.

Makes 6 servings

3/4	cup catsup
1/2	cup brown sugar
2	tablespoons lite soy sauce
1	tablespoon apple cider vinegar
1	green pepper, diced
6	chicken breast halves, boned, skinned, and cut into 1/2-inch slices
2	cups diced fresh pineapple

Put catsup, sugar, soy sauce, and vinegar into a pan. Cook mixture until sugar is dissolved. Stir in pepper and chicken and cook until chicken is done, about 20 minutes. Stir occasionally. Add pineapple and let heat up. Serve with rice.

❖

Each serving provides:

282	Calories	22 g	Carbohydrate
28 g	Protein	639 mg	Sodium
2 g	Fat	68 mg	Cholesterol
2 g	Dietary Fiber		

Chicken and Rice Curry Stew

Here is a delicious curry dish. If you like curry, try cooking with curry paste. It is smooth and blends easily into dishes.

Makes 6 servings

3	whole chicken breasts, boned, skinned, and cut in 1 1/2-inch squares
	vegetable spray
1 1/2	cups rice
3	green onions, sliced
1	clove garlic, minced
1	carrot, grated
5	small dried apricots, minced
3	tablespoons dried cranberries
1/4	teaspoon allspice
1	tablespoon curry powder (or more, to taste)
3	cups chicken stock, defatted (see page 6)
1	cup fruit stock (see page 15)
1/2	cup sherry
	salt and pepper to taste
1/4	cup slivered almonds for garnish

Preheat oven to 350°.

Sauté chicken until it just begins to brown, in a Dutch oven pan sprayed with vegetable spray. Add all other ingredients to the pan except the almonds, salt, and pepper, and mix well.

Bring stew to a boil on top of the stove and then put into oven for 30 to 35 minutes. Remove from oven and fluff rice. Season with salt and pepper and garnish with slivered almonds.

❖

Each serving provides:

410	Calories	59 g	Carbohydrate
33 g	Protein	240 mg	Sodium
4 g	Fat	70 mg	Cholesterol
4 g	Dietary Fiber		

TURKEY MEATBALL STEW

My father and mother-in-law, Elmo and Valerie Ferrari, owned a home in Napa where they grew Italian beans. They are my favorite, but in most markets you can only find them frozen and they are so much better fresh. Of course, you can substitute fresh green beans instead of frozen Italian if you don't have the Italian fresh.

Makes 8 servings

1	pound lean ground turkey breast
1/2	cup old-fashioned oats
2	egg whites
4	green onions, sliced
1/2	cup minced red pepper
1/2	teaspoon salt and fresh ground pepper
2	cloves garlic, minced
1/4	cup nonfat milk
	vegetable spray
1	medium onion, chopped
2	teaspoons unsalted butter
2	tablespoons flour mixed with 1/3 cup very hot water
2	cups chicken stock, defatted (see page 6)
1	cup white wine
2	yams, peeled and diced
1/3	pound Italian beans (or any fresh green bean)
3	stalks celery, sliced
3	parsnips, peeled and diced
3	tablespoons chopped fresh parsley

1   teaspoon thyme
1   teaspoon ground sage
     salt and fresh ground pepper to taste

Preheat oven to 450°.

To make meatballs, mix first 8 ingredients. Shape into 1-inch balls and put on a cookie sheet sprayed with vegetable spray. Bake 25 to 30 minutes or until meatballs are browned. Set aside.

Sauté onion in butter for 5 minutes. Add flour mixture and mix well. Stir in chicken stock and wine and stir until smooth. Add meatballs, yams, Italian beans, celery, parsnips, parsley, thyme, and sage. Cook 40 minutes, or until vegetables are done. Season with salt and pepper to taste.

❖

Each serving provides:

240	Calories	34 g	Carbohydrate
17 g	Protein	342 mg	Sodium
3 g	Fat	33 mg	Cholesterol
5 g	Dietary Fiber		

CRANBERRY BEANS with JALAPEÑO STEW

If you cannot find cranberry beans in your market, try your local farmers' markets.

Makes 12 servings

1	pound cranberry beans
1	pound ground turkey
	vegetable spray
1	cup chopped onion
1/2	cup chopped carrot
1/2	cup chopped celery
2	jalapeño peppers, minced
2	cloves garlic, minced
1	teaspoon chili sauce (or to taste)
1	cup tomato sauce
5	tomatillos, papery skin removed and diced
1/2	teaspoon chili powder
1	teaspoon coriander seed
2	tablespoons minced cilantro
2	tablespoons Dijon mustard
4	cups chicken stock, defatted (see page 6)
2	zucchini, cut into 1/2-inch slices
	salt and pepper to taste

Pick over beans and soak overnight. Drain and set aside.

Sauté turkey in a nonstick pan sprayed with vegetable spray. Add onion, carrots, celery, jalapeño peppers, garlic, chili sauce, and tomato sauce and cook, stirring, for 10 minutes. Add beans, tomatillos, chili powder, coriander, cilantro, mustard, and stock. Cook 1 1/2 hours. Add zucchini and season with salt and pepper to taste. Cook 20 minutes more.

Each serving provides:

206	Calories	28 g	Carbohydrate
16 g	Protein	380 mg	Sodium
4 g	Fat	28 mg	Cholesterol
4 g	Dietary Fiber		

Drunken Chicken Stew

This was one of my mom's specialties—minus most of the fat.

Makes 6 servings

6	whole chicken breasts, boned, skinned, and cut into quarters
1/3	cup flour
	vegetable spray
3	large white rose potatoes, peeled and diced large
1	small onion, cut into thin wedges
2	tablespoons flour mixed with 1/4 cup hot water
4	celery stalks, cut into 2-inch pieces
3	carrots, peeled and cut diagonally into 1/2-inch slices
1/2	cup chopped fresh parsley
1	teaspoon thyme
1 1/2	teaspoons vegetable seasoning (such as Vegit®)
1	cup white wine
3	cups chicken stock, defatted (see page 6)
1/4	cup whiskey (optional)
	fresh ground pepper and salt to taste

Dip chicken pieces in flour and shake off excess. Spray a non-stick sauté pan with vegetable spray and sauté chicken until it is lightly browned. Set chicken aside.

Sauté potatoes and onion for 3 minutes in the same pan with a little more vegetable spray. Stir in flour and water mixture.

Return chicken to pan. Add celery, carrots, parsley, thyme, vegetable seasoning, wine, and chicken stock and cook covered for 30 minutes. Add whiskey, and pepper and salt to taste. Simmer, uncovered for 5 more minutes.

❖

Each serving provides:

407	Calories	27 g	Carbohydrate
58 g	Protein	339 mg	Sodium
4 g	Fat	138 mg	Cholesterol
4 g	Dietary Fiber		

Chicken and Asparagus Delight

I can never wait for spring to arrive—and for those beautiful spears of asparagus to show up at all the farmers' markets.

Makes 8 servings

1/2	cup sliced green onion
2	cloves garlic, minced
1/8	teaspoon red pepper flakes
2	teaspoons butter
3	whole chicken breasts, boned, skinned, and diced large
1	tablespoon flour mixed with 1/3 cup boiling water
1/2	cup dry white wine
2	cups chicken stock, defatted (see page 6)
1	tablespoon chopped fresh tarragon
1	cup sliced celery
1	teaspoon white pepper
2	ounces wide egg noodles
4	cups 1-inch dice asparagus
	salt to taste

Sauté onion, garlic, and red pepper flakes in butter until onion is soft. Add chicken and cook until pink color is gone. Mix flour and boiling water until well blended. Whisk into wine and stock. Add to pan with chicken, blending well. Add tarragon, celery, and pepper and cook, covered, 15 minutes. Add noodles, stir well, and cook, covered, 5 minutes more. Add asparagus and cook uncovered until asparagus is done, about 10 minutes. Season with salt to taste.

❖

Each serving provides:

176	Calories	12 g	Carbohydrate
25 g	Protein	236 mg	Sodium
3 g	Fat	62 mg	Cholesterol
2 g	Dietary Fiber		

Sweet and Fruity Chicken Stew

In this stew, fruit pairs up with chicken for a delightful change of pace.

Makes 8 servings

1	small onion, diced
1	large Granny Smith apple, peeled and diced
1	tablespoon brown sugar
	juice of 1 lemon
2	teaspoons lemon rind
1/2	cup sangria (Spanish fruit wine)
1 1/2	cups chicken stock, defatted (see page 6)
8	chicken breast halves, boned and skinned
1	8-ounce can unsweetened apricot halves with their juice
2	teaspoons cornstarch mixed with 3 tablespoons water
	salt to taste

Preheat oven to 350°.

Put onion, apple, sugar, lemon juice, and lemon rind into a pan and cook on low heat until liquid is evaporated and onion is a nice brown color. Add sangria, stock, and chicken. Cook, covered, in oven about 25 minutes. Remove from oven. Put apricots and their juice into a pan and stir in cornstarch mixture. Warm until thickened. Stir apricot mixture into chicken, just to blend, then serve. Salt to taste.

❖

Each serving provides:

172	Calories	9 g	Carbohydrate
28 g	Protein	81 mg	Sodium
2 g	Fat	69 mg	Cholesterol
1 g	Dietary Fiber		

Chicken with Cabbage and Parsnips

This is warming stew for a cold winter's night.

Makes 6 servings

6	chicken breast halves, boned, skinned, and cut in half
	vegetable spray
3	leeks, white part only, sliced
2	cloves garlic, minced
2	tablespoons flour mixed with 1/2 cup boiling water
3	cups chicken stock, defatted (see page 6)
3	potatoes, peeled and diced
1	cup diced celery
1	teaspoon caraway seed
1	teaspoon dried thyme
1/4	teaspoon liquid smoke flavoring
1	teaspoon white pepper
2	cups diced cabbage
1	carrot, shredded
1	pound parsnips, peeled and sliced in 1 1/2-inch lengths
	salt to taste
	chopped fresh parsley for garnish

Sauté chicken in a pan sprayed with vegetable spray until the chicken browns. Remove chicken and set aside.

Sauté leeks and garlic for 2 minutes. Stir in flour and water mixture. Add stock and whisk until smooth. Add potatoes and celery and cook 20 minutes. Return chicken and add caraway seed, thyme, smoke flavoring, and pepper. Cook 15 minutes.

Add cabbage, carrots, and parsnips and cook about 8 minutes, or until parsnips are done. Season with salt and garnish with parsley.

❖

Each serving provides:

247	Calories	26 g	Carbohydrate
31 g	Protein	254 mg	Sodium
2 g	Fat	70 mg	Cholesterol
3 g	Dietary Fiber		

13

Fish
Stews

F ish and shellfish are excellent sources of protein and contain essential body fats that we all need. Omega-3 fatty acids, found in many fish, help fight heart disease and lower blood cholesterol levels. For all these reasons, we are told, we should try to eat fish at two to five meals a week. Luckily, fish merges well with many flavors and is delicious when submerged in spicy sauces.

Sometimes it is hard to determine if a dish is a stew or a soup. Some stews are in a light sauce and others are heavy and very thick. While many people classify gumbos and cioppinos as stews, I categorize them as soups. It is a very fine line to draw, and I really think it is insignificant—as long as we have a savory end result.

One of the conveniences of making stews is that they are long-cooking: they can be prepared and left to cook without fuss. Certain stews made with fish or chicken cannot cook for long periods of time or the meat will be tough and dry. Fortunately, the sauce for most of these fish stews improves dramatically with long, slow cooking. These sauces can be prepared the day before, or left to cook slowly all day in a Crock-pot; when your guests (or family) arrives, all that is left to do is add the fish right before serving.

Oriental Stew with Scallops

The chopping takes a little time, but it is worth it for this luscious Oriental dish.

Makes 4 servings

2	teaspoons sesame oil
3	cloves garlic, chopped
1	small onion, cut into thin wedges
1	green pepper, diced
1	teaspoon grated fresh ginger
1	tablespoon oyster sauce
1	teaspoon lite soy sauce
1/2	cup sake
3/4	cup fish stock (see page 14)
3/4	cup chicken stock (see page 6)
2	carrots, cleaned and thinly cut, diagonally
1/2	pound baby bok choy, white part only, sliced into wedges
3	green onions, sliced diagonally
6	Chinese black mushrooms, julienned and soaked in warm water
1	8-ounce can sliced bamboo shoots, drained
1	tablespoon cornstarch mixed with 2 tablespoons water
12	ounces scallops (cut in half if large)

Sauté garlic, onion, and pepper in sesame oil, 2 minutes. Add ginger, oyster sauce, soy sauce, sake, stocks, and carrots, and cook 10 minutes. Add bok choy, green onions, mushrooms, and bamboo shoots. Cook 5 minutes. Stir in cornstarch mixture and cook until thickened. Add scallops and cook for about 5 minutes more, or until scallops are tender.

❖

Each serving provides:

186	Calories	17 g	Carbohydrate
18 g	Protein	408 mg	Sodium
4 g	Fat	29 mg	Cholesterol
3 g	Dietary Fiber		

Halibut Delight

You can substitute any nice, white fish steaks for the halibut.

Makes 6 servings

1	pound halibut steaks
10	snow peas, julienned
2	stalks celery, julienned
2	carrots, julienned
3	green onions, julienned
1	large potato, julienned
8	ounces fish stock (see page 14) or clam juice
1/2	cup dry white wine
2	tomatoes, peeled and chopped
2	tablespoons chopped fresh parsley
1	tablespoon chopped fresh dill
2	shallots, minced
2	cloves garlic, minced
1	hot red pepper, minced
2	tablespoons flour mixed with 1/4 cup water
	salt and pepper to taste

Cut halibut into 1 1/2-inch pieces and set aside. Cut all vegetables julienne-style and put potatoes in a bowl of cold water.

Put fish stock, wine, tomatoes, parsley, dill, shallots, garlic, peppers, and flour mixture into a pan. Blend well and cook 30 minutes. Add celery, carrots, and potatoes and cook 15 minutes more. Add halibut, green onions, and snow peas and cook until halibut is done and flakes, about 5 minutes. Season with salt and pepper to taste.

❖

Each serving provides:

147	Calories	13 g	Carbohydrate
18 g	Protein	198 mg	Sodium
2 g	Fat	24 mg	Cholesterol
2 g	Dietary Fiber		

Potato, Sole, and Vegetable Stew

Makes 8 servings

3	cloves garlic, minced
2	teaspoons butter
1	medium onion, diced
2	large potatoes, peeled and diced small
1	cup chicken stock, defatted (see page 6)
1	cup fish stock (see page 14)
1/3	cup dry vermouth
	juice of 1 lemon
1	teaspoon thyme
1	teaspoon chervil
1	bay leaf
1	10-ounce package frozen artichoke hearts, defrosted
3	carrots, peeled and sliced
2	cups asparagus, cut into 1-inch lengths
1 1/2	pounds sole, cut into 2-inch pieces
	salt to taste, lots of fresh ground pepper

Sauté onion and garlic in butter 2 minutes. Add potatoes, stocks, vermouth, lemon juice, thyme, chervil, and bay leaf. Cook 25 minutes. Add artichoke hearts, carrots, and asparagus

and cook 10 minutes more. Remove bay leaf and add sole.
Cook 5 minutes, or until fish flakes. Season with salt and lots of
fresh ground pepper.

❖

Each serving provides:

169	Calories	17 g	Carbohydrate
20 g	Protein	251 mg	Sodium
3 g	Fat	44 mg	Cholesterol
3 g	Dietary Fiber		

Fisherman's Stew

Make this stew when lots of fresh fish is available to you. Once you make your sauce, pick and choose your favorite types of fish to use.

Makes 10 servings

1	cup minced onion
2	cloves garlic, minced
1	red bell pepper, diced
1	tablespoon virgin olive oil
6	cups stewed tomatoes, crushed
2	cups fish stock (see page 14) or clam juice
1	cup dry vermouth
2	stalks celery, minced
2	tablespoons minced fresh basil
1	teaspoon oregano
1	teaspoon pepper
3	ounces spiral noodles
1	pound any combination of fish: sea bass, halibut, cod, or red snapper
1	pound shrimp, deveined and peeled
1	pound crab legs (or lobster or crawfish)
1/2	pound clams (or oysters or mussels)
	chopped fresh parsley for garnish

Sauté onion, garlic, and red bell pepper in olive oil, on low heat 5 minutes. Add tomatoes, stock, vermouth, celery, basil, oregano, and pepper. Cook mixture for 2 hours. Add noodles and cook 8 minutes. Add fish and cook 4 minutes. Add shrimp,

crab legs (or other choices), and clams (or other choices). Cook
5 minutes more. Season to taste with salt and garnish with
parsley.

❖

Each serving provides:

215	Calories	21 g	Carbohydrate
25 g	Protein	517 mg	Sodium
3 g	Fat	89 mg	Cholesterol
3 g	Dietary Fiber		

Catch-of-the-Day Stew

You would have a really good fishing day if you caught all this! The name of this recipe implies that you can substitute any fish you desire and it will taste great.

Makes 12 servings

1	cup chopped onion
4	cloves garlic, minced
	vegetable spray
6	tomatoes, peeled, seeded, and chopped
3	stalks celery, sliced
3	large potatoes, peeled and diced
1/4	cup chopped fresh parsley
2	tablespoons chopped fresh dill
1/2	teaspoon fennel seed
1	teaspoon chili sauce
1/4	teaspoon saffron
1	bay leaf
1/2	cup white wine
3	cups fish stock (see page 14)
1/2	pound cod, sea bass, *or* halibut
1/2	pound crawfish
1/2	pound prawns
1/2	pound scallops

Sauté onion and garlic in vegetable spray until onion is soft. Add tomatoes, celery, potatoes, parsley, dill, fennel seed, chili sauce, saffron, bay leaf, wine, and stock. Cook mixture 40 minutes. Remove bay leaf. Add white fish and cook 3 minutes. Add crawfish and prawns and cook 8 minutes more. Add scallops and cook for 5 more minutes.

Each serving provides:

133	Calories	12 g	Carbohydrate
17 g	Protein	105 mg	Sodium
1 g	Fat	76 mg	Cholesterol
2 g	Dietary Fiber		

Shellfish Stew

This is a stew to serve to good friends. Everyone will have great fun removing their fish from the shells. It is a little messy so make your dinner very casual and have lots of delicious bread to scoop up the sauce.

Makes 6 servings

5	cups fish stock (see page 14)
1	cup red wine
1	green pepper, chopped
1	red pepper, chopped
1/2	cup chopped celery
1/2	cup chopped carrot
3	leeks, white part only, sliced
4	cloves garlic, minced
2	cups chopped tomato, peeled and seeded
1/4	cup chopped fresh parsley
1	bay leaf
1	teaspoon Italian spice
1/4	teaspoon saffron
1	teaspoon sugar
2	yellow zucchini, diced
2	green zucchini, diced
2	large potatoes, peeled and diced
12	large prawns
2	lobster tails, cut into 3 pieces each
12	clams
12	mussels
	salt and pepper to taste
	arrowroot (optional, for thickening)

Put first 14 ingredients into a pan and cook on top of the stove
for 1 hour. Add zucchini and potatoes and cook 20 minutes
more, or until potatoes are done. Remove bay leaf and discard.
Season with salt and pepper.

Add prawns, cover, and cook 2 minutes. Add lobster and
cook 2 more minutes. Add other shellfish, cover pan, and cook
10 minutes more, or until shells open. Add salt and pepper to
taste. You may thicken this stew with arrowroot, but it is
scrumptious in large bowls with the sauce as is.

❖

Each serving provides:

277	Calories	23 g	Carbohydrate
35 g	Protein	515 mg	Sodium
3 g	Fat	146 mg	Cholesterol
4 g	Dietary Fiber		

Index

International Conversion Chart

These are not exact equivalents: they have been slightly rounded to make measuring easier.

LIQUID MEASUREMENTS

American	Imperial	Metric	Australian
2 tablespoons (1 oz.)	1 fl. oz.	30 ml	1 tablespoon
1/4 cup (2 oz.)	2 fl. oz.	60 ml	2 tablespoons
1/3 cup (3 oz.)	3 fl. oz.	80 ml	1/4 cup
1/2 cup (4 oz.)	4 fl. oz.	125 ml	1/3 cup
2/3 cup (5 oz.)	5 fl. oz.	165 ml	1/2 cup
3/4 cup (6 oz.)	6 fl. oz.	185 ml	2/3 cup
1 cup (8 oz.)	8 fl. oz.	250 ml	3/4 cup

SPOON MEASUREMENTS

American	Metric
1/4 teaspoon	1 ml
1/2 teaspoon	2 ml
1 teaspoon	5 ml
1 tablespoon	15 ml

WEIGHTS

US/UK	Metric
1 oz.	30 grams (g)
2 oz.	60 g
4 oz. (1/4 lb)	125 g
5 oz. (1/3 lb)	155 g
6 oz.	185 g
7 oz.	220 g
8 oz. (1/2 lb)	250 g
10 oz.	315 g
12 oz. (3/4 lb)	375 g
14 oz.	440 g
16 oz. (1 lb)	500 g
2 lbs	1 kg

OVEN TEMPERATURES

Farenheit	Centigrade	Gas
250	120	1/2
300	150	2
325	160	3
350	180	4
375	190	5
400	200	6
450	230	8

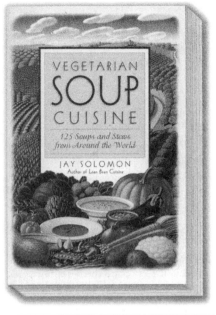

To Order Books

Please send me the following items:

Quantity	Title	Unit Price	Total
_____	The Once-a-Week Cooking Plan	$ 15.95	$ _____
_____	Spread Yourself Thin	$ 16.95	$ _____
_____	The Vegan Gourmet	$ 16.00	$ _____
_____	Vegetarian Soup Cuisine	$ 14.95	$ _____

Subtotal _____

7.25% Sales Tax (CA only) _____

7% Sales Tax (PA only) _____

5% Sales Tax (IN only) _____

7% G.S.T. Tax (Canada only) _____

Total Order _____

FREE
Ground Freight in U.S. and Canada

Foreign and all priority request orders:

Call Customer Service for a price quote at 800-632-8676

By Telephone: With American Express, MC, or Visa, call 800-632-8676. Mon–Fri, 8:30–4:30.

WWW: http://www.primapublishing.com

By E-mail: sales@primapub.com

By Mail: Just fill out the information below and send with your remittance to:

**Prima Publishing
3000 Lava Ridge Court
Roseville, CA 95661**

Name _____

Address_____

City _____ State _____ ZIP_____

American Express/MC/Visa# _____ Exp. _____

Check/money order enclosed for $_____ Payable to Prima Publishing

Daytime telephone _____

Signature _____